THE AFRICAN-AMERICAN KITCHEN

Angela Shelf Medearis

A DUTTON BOOK

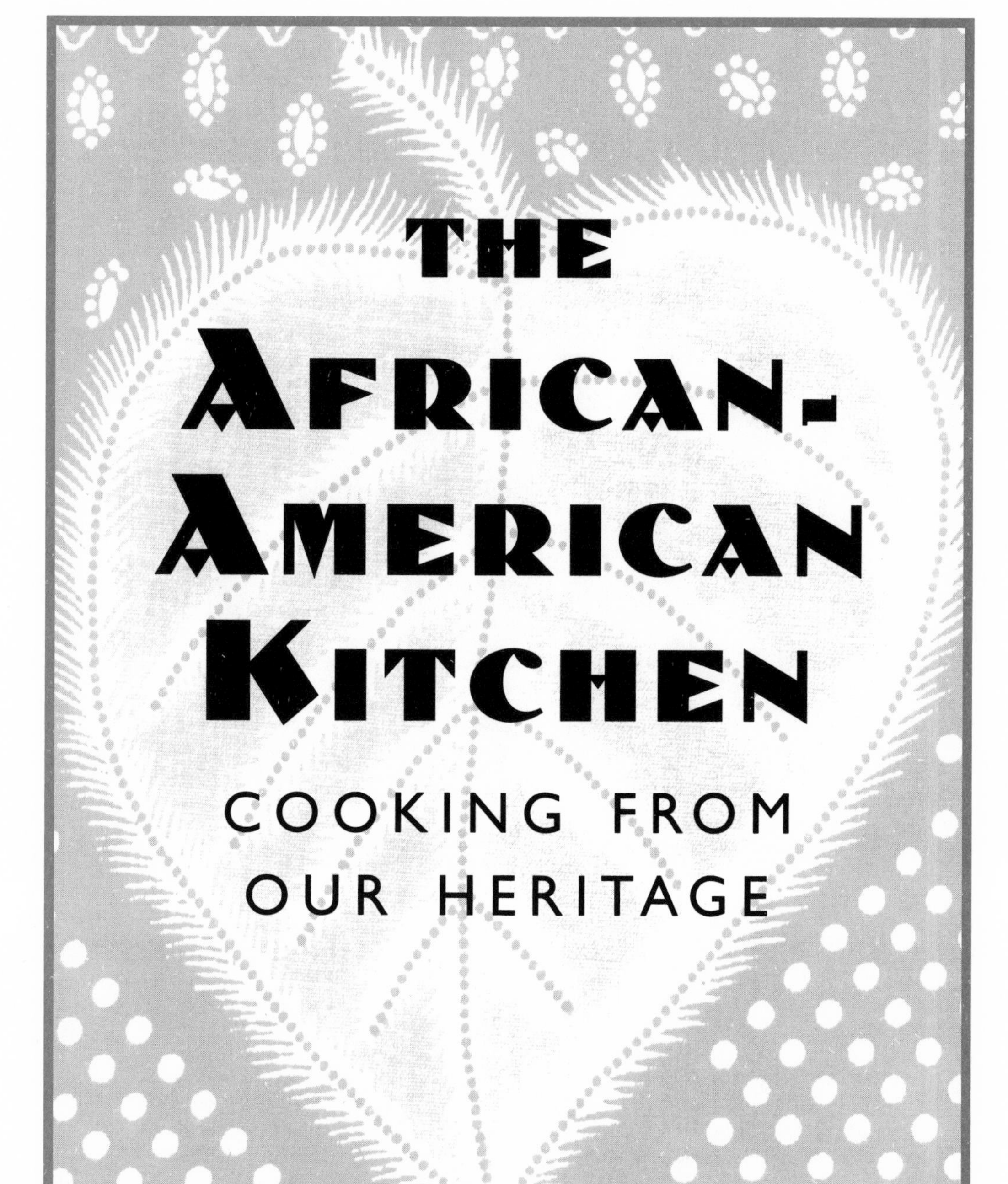
THE
AFRICAN-
AMERICAN
KITCHEN
COOKING FROM
OUR HERITAGE

DUTTON
Published by the Penguin Group
Penguin Books USA Inc., 375 Hudson Street, New York, New York 10014, U.S.A.
Penguin Books Ltd, 27 Wrights Lane, London W8 5TZ, England
Penguin Books Australia Ltd, Ringwood, Victoria, Australia
Penguin Books Canada Ltd, 10 Alcorn Avenue, Toronto, Ontario, Canada M4V 3B2
Penguin Books (N.Z.) Ltd, 182–190 Wairau Road, Auckland 10, New Zealand

Penguin Books Ltd, Registered Offices: Harmondsworth, Middlesex, England

First published by Dutton, an imprint of Dutton Signet, a division of Penguin Books USA Inc.
Distributed in Canada by McClelland & Stewart Inc.

First Printing, October, 1994
10 9 8 7 6 5 4 3 2

REGISTERED TRADEMARK—MARCA REGISTRADA

LIBRARY OF CONGRESS CATALOGING-IN-PUBLICATION DATA:
Medearis, Angela Shelf.
The African-American kitchen : cooking from our heritage / Angela Shelf Medearis.
p. cm.
ISBN 0-525-93834-6
1. Afro-American cookery. I. Title.
TX715.M48 1994
641.59'296073—dc20 94-1323
CIP

Printed in the United States of America
Set in Gill Sans
Designed by Eve L. Kirch

Dedicated to the memory
of my great-grandmother, Angeline Wilson Carolina,
and my grandmother, Willie Mae Davis

ACKNOWLEDGMENTS

With thanks to my mother, Angeline Shelf, and my sisters, Marcia Shelf and Sandra Fergins, for all their years of love, friendship, and food, and to Vivian Smyrl for her cheerful assistance.

Contents

Introduction xi

The Roots of Soul Cooking: Africa 1

The Pepper Pot Is Never Empty: The Caribbean 63

Making Do: Slave Kitchens 115

Getting Reacquainted: The African-American Kitchen 191

Holidays of Our Own: African-American Traditions 235

Index 247

Introduction

If my family had a coat of arms, at least one quadrant would have to be devoted to food. Perhaps a depiction of one of my grandfathers planting seeds or harvesting a crop, or my grandmothers cooking savory dishes in heavy black cast-iron skillets, or my entire family gathered around a heavily laden table eating, laughing, and talking, showing that special feeling of well-being that a good meal and good company give you.

This book contains some of the recipes that make up the cultural cooking heritage of many African-Americans. It is filled with authentic and historic recipes from West Africa, the West Indies, and Central America. It contains recipes from the U.S. South that were called receipts by slave cooks and their masters, and recipes that are a spicy blend of African, Latino, West Indian, European, and American foods. It's full of recipes that reflect the traditions and holidays at the foundation of African-American cooking and culture.

This cookbook began casually enough. My mother has a recipe for raisin-pecan pie that is unusual and a guaranteed diet-buster. She also has other recipes handed down through our family that while not unusual are simply wonderful. Some were hidden in musty, brittle old books; others were locked away in memory. The family wanted to make sure these recipes endured, and one of my sisters suggested a cookbook. Since I can both cook and write, I got the job.

When I started to think about how I would write this cookbook, I decided that it should be not only a way of preserving my family's recipes, but also a culinary exploration of my heritage. I wanted to examine the effect of slavery on the food, culture, and cooking techniques of the lands where Africans were enslaved. Many Africans were put to work as cooks, and they deserve much more credit for the way foods are seasoned and prepared than many cookbooks have given them. I also wanted to know why African-Americans traditionally eat what we eat and why we prepare our food the way we do. Along this culinary journey, I found foods, methods of preparation, and seasonings that linked the captive cooks from Africa to the Islands and to the Americas.

Historical African, Central American, American, and West Indian recipes form the heart of this book. The "receipts" from slave cooks form its soul. Ancient and modern, traditional and nontraditional cooking crafts are mixed to create the body of recipes contained in the African-American chapter. Each chapter is the beloved offspring of the preceding one, but all have roots in Africa.

I've found that my African ancestors left me intangible heirlooms—a will to survive, a strong sense of family, and a love of foods that connect me to the past. My unknown ancestors came with millions of others from the coasts of West, East, and South Africa—Senegal, Gambia, Sierra Leone, Ghana, Nigeria, Togo, Dahomey, the Ivory Coast, Cameroon, Gabon, Tanzania, Mali, Niger, Chad, Zaire, Angola, and Namibia—as well as a few countries in the continent's interior.

Stripped of every possession but their memories and their spirit, my ancestors survived the harrowing passage across the waters on a slave ship. The last remnant of home on this treacherous journey was the meals they received from their captors. Alexander Falconbridge, an English doctor who made several voyages on board slave ships, describes a typical meal in his 1788 narrative *Account of the Slave Trade on the Coast of Africa:*

> The diet of the Negroes while on board, consists chiefly of horsebeans [fava beans] boiled to the consistence of a pulp; of boiled yams and rice and sometimes of a small quantity of beef or pork. They [the sailors] sometimes make use of a sauce composed of palm-oil mixed with flour, water and red peppers, which the sailors call slabber-sauce. Yams are the favorite food of the Eboe or Bight Negroes, and

> rice or corn of those from the Gold and Windward Coasts; each preferring the produce of their native soil.

The African captives were taken as slaves to North, Central, and South America and the West Indies. They were severed forever from their homes and their old ways of life. They were given new names, forced to learn a new language and to labor under conditions that would have destroyed weaker spirits. They found few comforts in this strange new land. In their scant moments of privacy, they continued their African traditions—in language, music, religious customs, and foods. Finding foods similar to those in Africa and preparing them as they had been prepared in their homeland were a consolation to the captives, evoking warm memories of family, ceremonies, and feast days.

My African ancestors are an invisible but strong presence in my kitchen. Part of their legacy to me and to America can be found in a simmering pot of spicy okra gumbo, in a delicious handful of peanuts, in a steaming bowl of black-eyed peas and rice on a cold New Year's Day, and in freshly baked rolls, warm from the oven and covered with sesame seeds. African slaves introduced these four mainstays into the American diet—okra (which they called gombo), peanuts (which they called groundnuts or goobers), cowpeas or black-eyed peas, and sesame seeds (which they called benne) and the oil they produce. The African names for these foods are still used today. The seedlings for these and other crops were often transported from Africa on the slave ships. The African captives knew how to make the plants grow and how to cook and season the produce. African plants were cultivated by the slaves in the small gardens they were sometimes allowed to tend for their own use. The success of the early South Carolina rice crops was due in large part to the knowledge African slaves brought about the planting and cultivation of the grain.

I think of America as a stew. Each culture adds color, spice, taste, and texture to this country. Some aspects of the multitude of cultures which compose the base of this American stew have blended together harmoniously. Others still require years of cooking to make them tender and the sharp, spicy flavors compatible. From time to time, the mixture boils over furiously, leaving a scorched mess for future generations to clean up. When this American stew is simmering happily—all the cul-

tural flavors bubbling together in a broth of the best of each race—it is one of the most delicious experiences in the world.

There is a miraculous feeling that abides when family and friends gather together to share in a wonderful meal, and there is comfort in the ways of old. The contents of this book were my legacy; now they are yours as well.

Angela Shelf Medearis
Austin, Texas
November 1993

THE ROOTS OF SOUL COOKING

AFRICA

The man that eats no pepper is weak; pepper is the staff of life. —YORUBA PROVERB

Someone once asked me what made African dishes different from those of other countries. I thought for a moment. The answer came to me with scorching clarity: the temperature. Most African dishes are very hot! Peppers, whether mild, flavorful bell peppers or slender, blazing-hot cayenne peppers, are an essential ingredient in African cooking.

My first experience with African food was when a friend from Ghana lived with my family. Having graciously offered to prepare a traditional African dinner, she served us a tomato-based stew called palaver (also known as palava in different regions) which contained small portions of beef and spinach served over rice. It had a wonderful aroma, and we couldn't wait to try it. She warned us it was hot; we thought it would be like the Mexican dishes we're accustomed to from living in Texas, and assured her we were used to eating spicy foods. Several glasses of cold water later, we realized we were wrong! It was one of the hottest dishes any of us had ever attempted to eat. I found out later that the word *palaver*, which originated in West Africa, means "trouble."

Peppers give African dishes their distinctive flavor. The rule of thumb seems to be that the hotter the climate in Africa, the hotter the foods. A study conducted in 1954 found that eating the hotter kinds of peppers in warm climates causes a reaction called gustatory sweating. Unlike other types of perspiration, gustatory sweating

has a cooling effect on the body and is stimulated only by hot foods. The hotter the foods, the cooler the body.

I've learned to love African cooking. I've also learned to adjust the heat. The African recipes in this chapter use varying amounts of fresh and commercially prepared peppers. Some specify red peppers, others green chilies. Recipes that call for red peppers refer to the half-inch-long, fiery-hot red cayenne peppers. Recipes that call for green chilies refer to the mild five- to six-inch-long California or Anaheim chilies or, for those who prefer hotter dishes, the green, two- to three-inch-long jalapeño chilies. These chilies can be found in most grocery stores, dried, ground, canned, or fresh; you can use them in these recipes in any of these forms.

Remember always to wear gloves when preparing fresh peppers. Failure to do so will result in a burning sensation in your hands and any other part of your body you touch. Never use hot water to rinse dried or fresh peppers; it may send up fumes that will irritate your eyes and nose. You can crush dried peppers in a mortar and measure them out in this form.

When preparing fresh peppers, it's best to remove the stems and seeds with your gloved fingers. However, you can use a paring knife if the ribs of the pepper are thick and fleshy. Removing the seeds doesn't affect the flavor but greatly decreases the heat. Always wash your hands thoroughly with soap and cold water when you have finished preparing peppers. Be sure to clean any utensils or surfaces you have used.

African dishes are delicious and for the most part easy to prepare. Many of the recipes in this chapter hark back to Biblical times. I enjoy them because I feel that not only am I preparing a meal, I'm cooking a little bit of history.

SPICED OIL AND SAUCES

Níter Kebbeh

(Spícy Butter Oíl)

YIELD: 2 CUPS

This spicy cooking oil, similar to clarified butter, is used by Ethiopian cooks to add flavor to their food. Niter kebbeh is often used when preparing Doro We't (page 24).

4 sticks (1 pound) unsalted butter
3 tablespoons chopped garlic
1 small onion, chopped
¼ teaspoon crushed cardamom
4 teaspoons ground ginger
⅛ teaspoon ground nutmeg
1½ teaspoons ground turmeric
1 teaspoon ground cloves
1 cinnamon stick

Cut the butter into small pieces. In a heavy 4-quart saucepan, melt it over high heat until foamy. Be careful not to burn it. Stir in the garlic, onion, and spices. Reduce the heat to low but do not cover. Simmer the mixture for 45 minutes, stirring frequently.

Pour the mixture into a jar through a sieve lined with several layers of cheesecloth. Strain the oil repeatedly until it is clear. Any spices or solids that remain will turn the oil rancid. Cover the oil and store in the refrigerator for up to 6 months.

Berber and Taíney Sauce

YIELD: 1½ CUPS

This flavorful sauce is named for the North African Berber tribe famous for its tradition of horsemanship. Use the sauce to marinate or baste chicken and barbecued meats, or serve it at the table.

¼ cup raisins
4 tablespoons lemon juice
5 tablespoons butter, softened
⅔ cup peanut oil
3 teaspoons honey
1 tablespoon peanut butter
½ teaspoon curry powder
¼ teaspoon crushed red pepper flakes
¼ teaspoon dried basil
¼ teaspoon dried marjoram
¼ teaspoon ground allspice
Pinch chopped fresh mint

In a medium bowl, soak the raisins in the lemon juice for 15 minutes, or until plump. Add the butter, peanut oil, honey, peanut butter, and seasonings. Combine well. The sauce may be refrigerated for up to a week. The oil may separate, so stir well before using the sauce.

Ata Sauce
(Pepper Sauce)

YIELD: 1 CUP

Ata *is the Nigerian word for "hot." This sauce, excellent on baked or broiled meats, puts the bottled American type to shame.*

2 cups diced red bell pepper
1 large onion, diced
2 large tomatoes, sliced
½ teaspoon to 2 tablespoons crushed red pepper flakes, to taste
¼ teaspoon salt
½ cup peanut oil

Put the bell pepper, onion, tomatoes, red pepper flakes, and salt in a blender and pulse until coarsely chopped. In a heavy frying pan, heat the oil until it is hot but not smoking and sauté the mixture until the pepper is tender and the onion is golden brown. Simmer uncovered over low heat for 10 minutes, stirring occasionally.

APPETIZERS

South African Pickled Fish

YIELD: 4 SERVINGS

This wonderful appetizer must "pickle" for 2 days before it's ready to serve.

½ cup vegetable oil
2 pounds halibut fillets, about ½ inch thick

Marinade:

3 large onions, sliced ⅛ inch thick
½ cup packed light brown sugar
3 tablespoons chopped hot green chilies
1 tablespoon curry powder
1 tablespoon ground ginger
2 large bay leaves, crumbled, plus 2 whole bay leaves
1 teaspoon ground coriander
2 teaspoons salt
2 cups malt vinegar
1 cup water

In a heavy skillet over moderate heat, heat ¼ cup of the vegetable oil until it is hot but not smoking. Rinse the fillets in cool water and pat dry. Fry the fillets in the oil until golden brown, about 5 minutes on each side. Drain the fillets on paper towels until cool.

To prepare marinade: Discard the oil remaining in the skillet and wipe the skillet dry with paper towels. Heat the remaining oil until it is hot but not smoking. Add the onions and cook, stirring frequently, until they are golden brown. Add the sugar, chilies, curry powder, ginger, crumbled bay leaves, coriander, and salt. Cook over

low heat for 2 minutes, stirring frequently. Slowly stir in the vinegar and water and bring the mixture to a boil over high heat; reduce the heat to low and simmer the marinade, uncovered, for 10 minutes.

Remove any bones and skin from the fillets and cut them into 2-inch squares. Spread about a third of the halibut evenly in a 9 × 12-inch glass or enameled serving dish. Cover the halibut with a cup or so of the marinade, then add another layer of halibut, alternating the fish and marinade. Lay the whole bay leaves on top and cover the dish tightly with plastic wrap. Refrigerate for 2 days before serving.

Ghana Kelewele

(Plantain Appetizer)

YIELD: 6 SERVINGS

This appetizer is easy to prepare and makes a wonderful snack. In Ghana, kelewele is also served for breakfast and as a side dish, much like french fries.

2 cups cooking oil
2 tablespoons water
1 teaspoon ground ginger
½ teaspoon salt
½ teaspoon cayenne pepper
6 large unripened plantains, peeled and sliced ½ inch thick

In a deep-fryer or a skillet deep enough to cover the plantain slices, heat the oil until it is hot but not smoking.

In a small bowl, combine the water, ginger, salt, and cayenne pepper. Drop the plantain slices into the bowl one by one, coating each piece evenly.

Deep fry the plantain slices until golden brown. Drain on paper towels.

Kosaí/Akara Balls
(Bean Scoops)

YIELD: 4 SERVINGS

I love making kosai, or akara balls, as they're called in some parts of Africa. The traditional recipe calls for removing the skins from the black-eyed peas by soaking them overnight and then rubbing off the skins, but you lose many nutrients this way. Kosai taste great hot or cold.

1½ cups dried black-eyed peas
½ cup warm water
1 egg
½ teaspoon chili powder
½ teaspoon salt
½ teaspoon black pepper
1 cup grated onion
2 cups vegetable oil

In a blender, grind the peas for 3 minutes. Gradually add the water until the mixture turns into a paste. Scrape the bean paste into a bowl and whisk for 5 minutes to aerate the mixture. Add the egg, chili powder, salt, and pepper and beat again until the mixture is smooth. Mix in the onion.

In a deep-fryer or a deep skillet, heat the oil until it is hot but not smoking. Deep-fry tablespoonfuls of the bean mixture a few at a time until brown. Drain on paper towels.

VARIATIONS:

Akara Awon: Mix in ½ cup finely minced okra along with the onion.

Akara Meatballs: Add a second egg and 1 pound ground beef to the bean mixture.

Nigerian Eggplant Appetizer

YIELD: 4 SERVINGS

The eggplant and sesame seeds in this recipe make an unusual and nutritious dip for raw vegetables.

1 large eggplant, peeled and sliced
1 teaspoon sesame seeds
1 clove garlic
½ teaspoon salt
4 tablespoons lemon juice
2 tablespoons chopped parsley

Bake the eggplant in a 350-degree oven about 10 minutes or microwave on high 5 to 7 minutes, until tender. In a blender, grind the sesame seeds and garlic into a paste. Add the eggplant and blend until smooth. Blend in the salt and lemon juice. Mound the dip on a shallow dish and sprinkle with the chopped parsley.

Nigerian Curry Dip

YIELD: 1 CUP

If you're not accustomed to the extra kick curry gives to food, you may want to add ½ tablespoon of the seasoning at a time until it suits your taste. Serve this dip with raw vegetables.

1 cup mayonnaise
2 tablespoons prepared salsa
½ to 2 tablespoons curry powder
1 tablespoon Worcestershire sauce
1 tablespoon grated onion
1 clove garlic
¼ teaspoon salt
¼ teaspoon black pepper

Blend all the ingredients until well combined. Chill.

Hummus

(Sesame Dipping Sauce)

YIELD: 6 SERVINGS

Sesame seeds are tiny but are full of protein, amino acids, calcium, and phosphorus—as well as flavor. Sesame is probably one of the oldest vegetations grown for oil and was introduced to the New World by African slaves. In Africa, sesame is called benne (BEHN-ee) or simsim. Africans considered the tiny seeds good-luck charms. In African cooking, sesame seeds are added to everything from main dishes to desserts. Serve this sesame dip with raw vegetables or crackers.

1 16-ounce can chickpeas, drained
1 clove garlic, peeled
4 teaspoons sesame seeds
2 teaspoons lemon juice
½ teaspoon salt
½ teaspoon butter, softened

Put the chickpeas and garlic in a blender and grind until smooth. Scrape the mixture into a bowl and add the remaining ingredients, mixing well.

SALADS

Lesotho Mealie Meal Salad

YIELD: 5 SERVINGS

This recipe from Lesotho uses mealie meal (cornmeal), the staple crop of this South African enclave. Slice the loaf and serve it cold, on a bed of lettuce, with dollops of mayonnaise.

1½ cups mealie meal (cornmeal)
4 cups boiling water
2 carrots
2 eggs
1 medium onion, finely minced
2 small tomatoes, chopped
1 teaspoon salt
1 teaspoon black pepper
Pinch cayenne pepper

In a large mixing bowl, stir the cornmeal and the boiling water together until smooth, about 5 minutes. Allow the mixture to cool. Boil the carrots and eggs together until the carrots are tender and the eggs are hard-cooked, about 10 minutes. Shell the eggs and chop them with the carrots, onion, and tomatoes until fine. Combine the egg and vegetable mixture with the cornmeal paste. Season with the salt and pepper. Pat the mixture into a lightly buttered loaf pan. Refrigerate until ready to serve.

South African Date and Onion Salad

YIELD: 4 SERVINGS

This salad makes a delightful contrast to a spicy main dish.

3 tablespoons red-wine vinegar
½ teaspoon salt
¼ teaspoon sugar
8 ounces pitted dates, quartered
1 medium onion, thinly sliced

In a medium serving bowl, stir together the vinegar, salt, and sugar until the sugar is completely dissolved. Add the dates and onion and stir until they are evenly coated. Refrigerate in an airtight container. This salad is best when served within 24 hours of preparation.

Orange Salad

YIELD: 6 SERVINGS

This refreshing salad, common to North Africa, is simple to prepare.

2 cups iceberg lettuce, shredded
1 large onion, thinly sliced
8 Greek olives, pitted and chopped
2 large oranges, peeled and thinly sliced

Dressing:

2 tablespoons olive oil
2 tablespoons lemon juice
⅛ teaspoon salt
Pinch cayenne pepper

Toss the lettuce, onion, and olives in a salad bowl. Arrange the orange slices on top.

Whisk together the oil, lemon juice, salt, and cayenne pepper and drizzle over the salad. Refrigerate until ready to serve.

South African Cucumber and Chili Salad

YIELD: 6 SERVINGS

Before eating, open thy mouth. —Wolof proverb

2 large cucumbers, peeled and thinly sliced
1½ teaspoons salt
3 tablespoons red-wine vinegar
½ teaspoon sugar
1 teaspoon finely chopped fresh hot green chili

In a bowl, combine the cucumbers, salt, 1 tablespoon of the vinegar, and ¼ teaspoon of the sugar. Marinate the mixture for 30 minutes at room temperature. Using a paper towel, squeeze the excess moisture out of the cucumbers and remove them to a serving bowl. Combine the cucumbers with the remaining 2 tablespoons of vinegar, the remaining ¼ teaspoon of sugar, and the chilies. Toss until the cucumbers are thoroughly coated.

Yemíser Selatta
(Ethíopían Lentíl Salad)

YIELD: 4 SERVINGS

In Ethiopia, lentil salad is traditionally served during Lent, either alone or with Ethiopian Injera Bread (page 56).

1¼ cups (about ½ pound) dried lentils
3 tablespoons red-wine vinegar
2 tablespoons vegetable oil
1 teaspoon salt
¼ teaspoon black pepper
8 large shallots, peeled and halved lengthwise
1 fresh hot green chili, stemmed, seeded, and julienned

Wash the lentils in a sieve under cold running water. Bring to a boil a medium pot of water to which you have added a pinch of salt. Add the lentils. The water should cover them by 2 or 3 inches. Partly cover the pot. Simmer for 25 to 30 minutes, or until the lentils are firm but tender. Drain the lentils in a sieve, cool them under cold running water, drain them again, and set them aside.

In a deep bowl, combine the vinegar, oil, salt, and pepper. Whisk until well blended. Stir in the lentils, shallots, and chili until they are well coated. Marinate the salad at room temperature for at least 30 minutes, stirring gently from time to time.

AN AFRICAN JAM AND A CONDIMENT

East African Banana Jam

YIELD: ABOUT 3 CUPS

This jam is wonderful with bread or as a cake filling. Aluminum utensils react with the lemon juice and bananas, so use stainless steel, wooden, plastic, or enamel utensils when preparing this dish.

6 ripe medium bananas
2 cups sugar
½ cup lemon juice
1 tablespoon lemon zest

Slice the bananas into ¼-inch rounds. In a large nonreactive bowl, stir together the sugar, lemon juice, and lemon zest until the sugar dissolves. Fold in the banana slices until evenly coated. Cover the bowl with plastic wrap or foil and let the bananas marinate at room temperature for at least 1 hour.

Put the bananas and marinade in a saucepan. Bring to a boil, stirring frequently. Reduce the heat to very low and simmer, uncovered, for 30 minutes, stirring occasionally. The jam should be thick enough to mold with a spoon. Immediately ladle the jam into an airtight container and refrigerate.

African Carrot Sambal

YIELD: 6 SERVINGS

This condiment has a sweet and spicy flavor that goes well with a bowl of black beans.

8 medium carrots, scraped and coarsely grated
2 teaspoons salt
1 large green bell pepper, seeded and diced
1 small onion, minced
¼ cup red-wine vinegar
½ tablespoon cayenne pepper
1 teaspoon sugar

In a bowl, combine the carrots and salt. Let stand at room temperature about 30 minutes. Squeeze the carrots between paper towels to extract excess moisture and drain any liquid from the bowl. In a separate bowl stir together the bell pepper, onion, vinegar, pepper, and sugar until the sugar is completely dissolved. Add the carrots and gently blend. Let the carrots marinate at room temperature for 15 minutes before serving.

STEWS AND SOUPS

Palava Stew

YIELD: 8 TO 10 SERVINGS

Palava stew was my first introduction to African food. It has a wonderful flavor. Palava is usually served with a side dish like Rice Foofoo (page 54). For a delightful change, substitute smoked turkey for the chicken.

1 pound stew beef, cut into 1½-inch chunks
1 pound dark meat chicken, cut at joints
1 teaspoon salt
1 teaspoon curry powder
½ teaspoon cayenne pepper
½ cup peanut oil
1 large onion, thinly sliced
4 cups water
½ cup sliced okra
1½ cups packed chopped spinach
1½ cups packed chopped mustard greens
1 cup sliced mushrooms

Sprinkle the beef and chicken with the salt, curry powder, and cayenne pepper. In a Dutch oven, heat the oil until it is hot but not smoking, add the onion and brown the beef and chicken a few pieces at a time. Pour off any remaining oil. Return all the beef and chicken to the pot and add the remaining ingredients. Cover and bring to a boil over high heat. Reduce the heat to low and simmer, stirring occasionally, for 20 minutes, or until the vegetables are tender and the meat is thoroughly cooked.

Groundnut Stew

YIELD: 8 SERVINGS

In Africa peanuts are called groundnuts. This is one of the most popular stews on the continent. It is delicious when served with brown rice, Rice Foofoo (page 54), or Ghana Kelewele (page 10).

2 tablespoons peanut or vegetable oil
1 3½- to 4-pound chicken, cleaned and cut up, or 6 whole bone-in chicken breasts
2 cloves garlic, minced
½ pound medium shrimp, shelled and deveined
1 6-ounce can tomato paste, mixed with 2 cups water
½ teaspoon curry powder
½ teaspoon dried thyme
Cayenne pepper to taste
⅔ cup chunky-style peanut butter

In a heavy pot or Dutch oven, heat the oil until it is hot but not smoking. Reduce the heat to moderate. Add the chicken, cooking a few pieces at a time so that the meat browns evenly. Remove it from the pot when browned. When all the chicken is browned, drain off all but 2 tablespoons of the fat in the pot. Add the garlic and shrimp and stir until the garlic is golden and the shrimp are done, about 2 minutes.

Add the tomato paste mixture, curry powder, thyme, and cayenne pepper to the pot. Stir until the mixture is smooth. Let the stew simmer for 5 minutes. Remove 3 tablespoons of the stew liquid and mix it with the peanut butter until smooth. Slowly add the thinned peanut butter to the stew, stirring until it is well combined. Return the chicken pieces to the stewpot. Simmer the stew on low heat until the chicken is fork-tender, about 30 minutes.

Doro We't

YIELD: 6 SERVINGS

Doro We't is a very popular Ethiopian stew. It is usually served on special occasions and has several variations, with meat and without. Ethiopian Injera Bread (page 56), the pancake-like national bread, is always served with Doro We't and is used to absorb every drop of the flavorful sauce.

- **1 3½- to 4-pound chicken, cleaned, skinned, and cut into 8 pieces**
- **1 lime, quartered**
- **1 cup butter or Niter Kebbeh (page 5)**
- **1 red onion, chopped**
- **½ teaspoon cayenne pepper**
- **2 cups water**
- **¼ teaspoon ground cardamom**
- **2 teaspoons garlic powder**
- **½ teaspoon ground ginger**
- **1 teaspoon salt**
- **¼ teaspoon black pepper**
- **6 medium hard-cooked eggs, sliced**

In a bowl, soak the chicken pieces in water to cover. Gently squeeze the juice from the quartered lime over the chicken and add the lime pieces to the bowl. Set aside.

In a skillet, melt the butter or heat the Niter Kebbeh over low heat and sauté the onion until golden brown. Add the cayenne pepper and increase the heat to moderate. Add the water, cardamom, garlic powder, and ginger to the skillet. Stir well and add the chicken pieces. Cook about 30 minutes, stirring occasionally, until the chicken is tender. Do not overcook. Sprinkle in the salt and stir. Remove the chicken from the skillet and place in a serving bowl. Pour the sauce over the chicken and sprinkle with the black pepper. Arrange the hard-cooked eggs on top.

Lamb Taushe

YIELD: 6 SERVINGS

Taushe is a stew served in most parts of Africa. You can substitute beef for the lamb if you desire.

¼ cup vegetable oil
2 pounds boneless stew lamb
1 large tomato, peeled and chopped
1 teaspoon salt
1 large onion, diced
4 scallions, chopped
½ tablespoon black pepper
2 cups water
1¼ cups diced pumpkin meat (about 1 pound)
¼ cup peanut butter
½ pound spinach, washed and shredded

In a large, heavy pot, heat the oil until it is hot but not smoking and brown the lamb. Add the tomato, salt, onion, scallions, pepper, and water. Simmer for 30 minutes. Add the pumpkin and simmer for another 20 minutes. Add the peanut butter and spinach and simmer for an additional 20 minutes, or until the vegetables are tender.

Muhogo Tamu
(East African Beef and Cassava Stew)

YIELD: 6 SERVINGS

Cassava or manioc, the tuber from which tapioca is made, is one of the African continent's staple foods. Cassava is cooked whole, pounded into a pulp, or ground into a coarse flour, which is used to make gari. Gari is especially popular in Ghana and other parts of West Africa. It has a slightly sour taste and, like rice, for which it often acts as a substitute, swells to twice its size when soaked in water. Instant Cream of Wheat can sometimes be substituted for gari.

As the African captives traveled, cassava has traveled too. It is known as farinhe de mandioca *in Brazil, and is commonly used in dishes of the West Indies. Cassava is a tasty way to thicken soups and stews, and provides a nutritious starch when served as a side dish. Some American grocery stores stock cassava, and you can often find it both whole and powdered in Asian markets.*

1½ teaspoons salt
1 pound cassava, peeled and cut into ½-inch cubes
1½ pounds stew beef, cubed
1 teaspoon black pepper
¼ cup peanut oil
1 small onion, minced
1 teaspoon ground turmeric
2 medium tomatoes, cut into wedges
1 cup water
1 cup coconut milk
1 tablespoon chopped hot fresh green chili
3 tablespoons chopped cilantro

Fill a medium pot with water and add ½ teaspoon of the salt. Bring the water to a boil and add the cassava. Boil the cassava until it is fork-tender but not mushy, about 10 minutes. Drain in a colander and set aside.

Season the stew meat with the remaining salt and the pepper. In a skillet, heat the oil until it is hot but not smoking and brown the beef over moderate heat, turning frequently. Drain on paper towels. Add the onion to the oil that remains in the pan and cook, stirring frequently, until golden brown. Add the turmeric and cook, stirring for 1 minute.

Return the beef to the skillet. Add the tomatoes and water and combine all the ingredients well. Increase the heat to high and bring the mixture to a boil. Reduce the heat to low and simmer, partly covered, about 1 hour, or until the beef is tender.

In a bowl, combine the coconut milk, chili, and cilantro and pour the mixture into the skillet. Add the cassava and combine all the ingredients well. Simmer, partly covered, 10 to 15 minutes.

Froí

(Ghanían Eggplant Stew)

YIELD: 4 SERVINGS

In Africa eggplants are often called garden eggs. Eggplant and fish make a tasty combination. The tablespoon of poultry seasoning may sound strange; however, I've found that it's a wonderful flavoring for fish. After all, taste is the true test of any meal.

2 pounds fish fillets (any white fish such as sole or flounder)
1 tablespoon poultry seasoning
3 tablespoons olive oil
1 large eggplant, peeled and cut into ½-inch cubes
½ cup chopped onion
½ cup chopped green bell pepper
2 tomatoes, quartered
½ tablespoon salt
¼ teaspoon crushed red pepper flakes
½ teaspoon black pepper
1 cup water
½ pound shrimp, shelled and deveined

Preheat the oven to 350 degrees.

Wash the fillets and pat dry. Sprinkle with the poultry seasoning; set aside.

In a heavy skillet, heat the oil until it is hot but not smoking, and cook the eggplant, onion, bell pepper, and tomatoes over moderate heat until the onions are soft but not brown. Add the salt, red pepper flakes, and pepper. Reduce the heat to low, cover the skillet tightly, and simmer until the vegetables are tender, about 5 minutes. Put the vegetables in a blender or food processor and puree until smooth.

Pour the pureed vegetables into a 6-quart casserole or Dutch oven. Layer the fillets over the vegetables and arrange the shrimp over the fillets. Add the water, cover tightly, and bake for 30 minutes.

Congo Green Papaya Soup

YIELD: 4 SERVINGS

Papayas are also known as pawpaws and tree melons. Green papayas are good for soups, pickles, and chutneys. Papayas can be eaten raw after they have become fairly soft and the skin has turned from green to yellow.

2 chicken bouillon cubes
2 cups boiling water
2 tablespoons butter or margarine
1 small onion, minced
2 large green papayas, peeled, sliced lengthwise, seeded, and diced (about 2 cups)
1 teaspoon salt
¼ teaspoon cayenne pepper
¼ cup milk
1 teaspoon cornstarch

Dissolve the bouillon cubes in the water and set aside. In a saucepan, melt the butter or margarine. Add the onion and sauté until it is transparent, then add the bouillon. Add the papaya, salt, and cayenne pepper to the chicken bouillon and simmer until the papaya is tender, about 8 minutes. Pour the mixture into a blender or food processor and puree until smooth, then return it to the saucepan. Pour the milk into a small bowl and slowly add the cornstarch, stirring until smooth. Add the cornstarch mixture to the papaya to thicken the soup. Simmer the soup over low heat, stirring constantly, for 5 minutes.

Efo

(Nigerian Spinach Soup)

YIELD: 8 SERVINGS

If one wants to catch a large fish, he must give something to the stream.

—Dahomean proverb

- **1 pound fish fillets (any type of white fish such as catfish, sole, or flounder)**
- **2 cups water**
- **¼ teaspoon salt**
- **¼ cup peanut oil**
- **1 large onion, diced**
- **2 medium tomatoes, diced**
- **¼ teaspoon dried thyme**
- **¼ teaspoon cayenne pepper**
- **1½ pounds spinach, washed and shredded**
- **½ pound shrimp, shelled and deveined**

Cut the fish fillets into small pieces and place them in a large uncovered pot. Add the water and salt. Simmer the fish until the water partially evaporates, about 10 minutes, then add the peanut oil, onion, tomatoes, thyme, and red pepper flakes. Simmer for 5 minutes, then add the spinach and shrimp. Do not add any more water unless the mixture begins to stick. Cook over low heat for 20 minutes, stirring occasionally, until the spinach is tender.

MAIN DISHES

Moroccan Beef Tagine with Artichokes

YIELD: 6 SERVINGS

Tagine means a type of casserole, as well as the earthenware dish the meal is cooked and served in. Tagines are traditionally simmered over low heat to allow enough time for the spices to mingle to perfection.

3 tablespoons olive oil
2 pounds stew beef, cubed
1 medium onion, chopped
2 medium tomatoes, sliced
1 teaspoon salt
½ teaspoon ground ginger
½ teaspoon black pepper
¼ cup chopped parsley
¼ teaspoon ground cinnamon
1½ cups beef broth
12 fresh artichoke hearts (or 2 10-ounce packages frozen artichoke hearts or 1 8-ounce jar artichoke hearts)

In a skillet, hear the oil until it is hot but not smoking and brown the beef. Add the onion and cook over moderate heat until golden. Add the tomatoes and seasonings. Reduce the heat and simmer for 25 minutes, stirring occasionally. Add the broth and artichoke hearts and simmer until the artichoke hearts are tender (about 30 minutes if you use fresh, 15 to 20 minutes if you use frozen or canned).

Chicken Tagine with Almonds

YIELD: 4 SERVINGS

Rooster, do not be so proud. Your mother was only an eggshell. —Ashanti proverb

5 tablespoons butter or margarine
4 tablespoons olive oil
1 clove garlic, crushed
¼ teaspoon ground ginger
⅛ teaspoon ground saffron
½ cup water plus additional as needed
1 2- to 3-pound chicken, quartered
1 teaspoon ground coriander
¼ cup sliced almonds

In a skillet, melt 4 tablespoons of the butter or margarine. Add the oil, garlic, ginger, and saffron and cook briefly over moderate heat until the garlic is golden. Slowly add ½ cup of the water to the sauce in the skillet, then add the chicken pieces. Add water until the chicken is partly covered. Add the coriander and cover the skillet. Reduce the heat to low and simmer until the chicken is tender, about 45 minutes. Remove the chicken from the skillet and arrange on a serving dish.

Increase the heat to high and boil the sauce until reduced by half, stirring frequently. Pour the sauce over the chicken. In a small pan over moderate heat, melt the remaining tablespoon of butter or margarine. Add the almonds and cook until browned, about 3 minutes. Sprinkle the browned almonds over the chicken.

Moushkakí

(Somalí Barbecue)

YIELD: 4 SERVINGS

Somalia was just a distant place on the map to me until American troops were sent there to assist the Somalis during their country's time of war and famine. Somalis are traditionally a nomadic people, and this recipe reflects that. Moushkaki is easy to prepare and can be cooked over an open fire.

½ cup lemon juice, preferably fresh
1 clove garlic, crushed
½ teaspoon ground ginger
½ teaspoon black pepper
¼ teaspoon cayenne pepper
1 teaspoon salt
2 pounds stew beef, cut into 1-inch cubes

In a bowl, combine all the ingredients except the beef. Add the beef, stir to coat, and refrigerate for 6 to 8 hours, stirring occasionally.

Place the beef on skewers and grill over charcoal that has become partly white with ash. Grill the beef until brown, turning frequently, about 10 to 15 minutes.

South African Bobotie

YIELD: 8 SERVINGS

Bobotie is a traditional meal for the Afrikaners (South Africans of European, usually Dutch, ancestry). It is similar to American meat loaf and is usually served with rice. The heavy East Indian influence in this dish is the result of the Dutch slave trade in Malaysia. The African traders brought East Indian spices back to Africa, and the slave cooks used the spices and cooking techniques they were familiar with to create a new cuisine in the country where they were enslaved.

2 slices firm white bread, crumbled
2 cups milk
1½ pounds ground beef
2 medium onions, chopped
1 clove garlic, minced
2 tablespoons butter
1½ teaspoons curry powder
1 teaspoon salt
1 tablespoon sugar
2 tablespoons lemon juice
½ teaspoon lemon zest
2 tablespoons raisins
2 tablespoons sliced almonds
2 tablespoons apricot jam
2 eggs

Preheat the oven to 350 degrees.

Soak the bread in 1 cup of the milk for 5 minutes. Squeeze out the excess liquid and in a large bowl combine the bread with the ground beef.

In a medium skillet, sauté the onions and garlic in 1 tablespoon of the butter until the onions are golden brown. Stir in 1 teaspoon of the curry powder, the salt, sugar, lemon juice, zest, raisins, almonds, and jam. Simmer the mixture for 15 minutes.

Add the mixture to the beef mixture in the bowl and blend in 1 egg. Put the mixture in a buttered baking dish, smoothing until flat, and bake for 30 minutes. Pour off the fat.

In a small bowl, combine the remaining egg, milk, and curry powder. Pour the mixture over the meat. Reduce the oven temperature to 300 degrees. Cook the bobotie until it is done and the topping is set, 30 to 40 minutes. Do not overcook, as bobotie should be moist.

Dodo and Síma

(Kenya Steak Supreme with Cornmeal Balls)

YIELD: 4 SERVINGS

The Kenyan steak dish called dodo is usually served smothered in tomato gravy and surrounded by sima, which are balls of cornmeal dough. It is truly a supreme meal.

Dodo:

- **2 tablespoons peanut oil**
- **1 pound sirloin steak, cut into 4 steaks**
- **1½ cups water**
- **1 tomato, peeled and chopped**
- **¼ teaspoon baking soda**
- **1 teaspoon salt**
- **½ teaspoon black pepper**
- **½ cup peanut butter**

Sima:

- **2 cups water**
- **1½ cups cornmeal**
- **1 tablespoon butter**
- **1 egg**
- **¼ cup milk**

In a skillet, heat the oil until it is hot but not smoking and brown the steaks on both sides. Remove the skillet from the heat. Add 1 cup of the water, the tomato, soda, salt, and pepper and return the skillet to the heat. Simmer until about ½ cup of liquid remains, 20 to 30 minutes.

In a small bowl, combine the peanut butter with the remaining ½ cup of water

until smooth. Add to the meat and simmer until the steak is tender, about 30 minutes.

To prepare the sima: In a saucepan, bring the water to a boil and slowly stir in the cornmeal. Reduce the heat to low and continue stirring until the cornmeal thickens. Add the butter and continue stirring, about 10 minutes, until the mixture is quite stiff. Remove from the heat. In a small bowl, beat together the egg and milk. Measure out tablespoons of the cornmeal dough and dip them in the egg mixture, placing each sima on a lightly greased cookie sheet. Brown the sima under a broiler for 2 to 3 minutes.

Arrange the dodo on a platter and surround it with the sima.

Yassa au Poulet
(West African Marinated Chicken)

YIELD: 4 SERVINGS

This wonderful West African dish is simmered in a savory lemon and onion marinade. Add a pot of rice and a green salad and you'll have a memorable meal.

2 cups sliced onion
3 cloves garlic, minced
½ teaspoon minced fresh hot green chili
½ teaspoon ground ginger
1 teaspoon white pepper
1 tablespoon salt
1 cup lemon juice
1¼ cups water
5 tablespoons peanut oil
1 2- to 3-pound chicken, quartered

In a large baking dish, combine the onion, garlic, chili, ginger, pepper, and salt. Stir in the lemon juice, 1 cup of the water, and 1 tablespoon of the oil. Coat the chicken pieces in the marinade, and refrigerate for at least 4 hours, turning the pieces every ½ hour.

Remove the chicken from the marinade, reserving the marinade, and pat the pieces dry with paper towels. In a skillet, heat the remaining 4 tablespoons of oil until it is hot but not smoking. Brown the chicken in the oil a few pieces at a time, turning frequently to brown evenly. Pour off all but about 2 tablespoons of oil from the skillet and remove it from the heat.

Using the back of a spoon, press the marinade through a fine sieve set over a bowl. Reheat the oil in the skillet and add the solids from the sieve. Stirring constantly, cook the onion until it is transparent, about 5 minutes.

Return the chicken to the skillet and add ½ cup of the strained marinade and the remaining ¼ cup of water. Bring to a boil over high heat. Partly cover the pan, reduce the heat, and simmer about 25 minutes, or until the chicken is tender.

Congo Chicken Moambe

YIELD: 4 SERVINGS

Chicken moambe has been called the national dish of the Congo. It has many variations. I like this version best because the seasonings blend so well. Serve it with rice.

1 3-pound chicken, quartered
1 teaspoon salt
½ teaspoon cayenne pepper
1 tablespoon butter
1 onion, minced
¼ teaspoon ground nutmeg
½ cup prepared tomato sauce
½ cup peanut butter

Season the chicken with the salt and cayenne pepper and put in a large pot. Cover the pieces with water, bring to a boil, and cook until tender, 45 to 55 minutes.

In a large saucepan, melt the butter and sauté the onion until golden brown. Add the nutmeg and tomato sauce and simmer about 5 minutes. Add the chicken and simmer over low heat, covered, about 15 minutes. Stir in the peanut butter and simmer for another 10 minutes.

Nigerian Roast Pepper Chicken

YIELD: 4 SERVINGS

The old woman looks after the hens and the hens look after the old woman [by laying eggs].
—Ashanti proverb

- **1 3-pound chicken, quartered**
- **½ cup peanut oil**
- **½ teaspoon cayenne pepper**
- **1 teaspoon salt, or to taste**
- **1 4-ounce jar pimentos, drained and diced**
- **1 onion, minced**
- **1 tomato, peeled and diced**

Preheat the oven to 400 degrees.

Brush the chicken pieces on both sides with the peanut oil, then season with the cayenne pepper and salt. Put the chicken in a baking dish and sprinkle with the pimentos, onion, and tomato. Bake until brown and done, 45 minutes to 1 hour.

Bamía

(Lamb with Okra)

YIELD: 4 SERVINGS

After eating, one's skin shines. [A person's successes are apparent.]

—Grebo people of Liberia

3 tablespoons olive oil
2 10-ounce packages frozen okra, thawed and drained
1 pound stew lamb, cut into 1-inch cubes
2 cloves garlic, chopped
2 to 3 medium tomatoes, peeled and chopped
1 teaspoon salt
½ teaspoon black pepper
1 cup water

In a saucepan, heat the oil until it is hot but not smoking. Add the okra and sauté until brown. Add the lamb, garlic, tomatoes, salt, pepper, and water. Cover, reduce the heat, and simmer about 1½ hours, until the lamb is tender.

East African Ham Kariba

YIELD: 8 SERVINGS

Few traditional African recipes use pork, so this recipe is probably a more modern African export. It makes a simple but filling meal.

2 large avocados
2 tablespoons lemon juice
3 medium tomatoes, thinly sliced
1 small onion, minced
1 hard-cooked egg, chopped
¼ cup chopped peanuts
1 small head lettuce, shredded
8 slices (12 ounces) ham, medium thickness

Dressing:

¼ cup mayonnaise
½ teaspoon salt
⅛ teaspoon cayenne pepper or more to taste

Peel the avocados and slice into bite-sized pieces and place in a bowl. Sprinkle the pieces with the lemon juice to prevent discoloration. Add the tomatoes, onion, egg, peanuts, and half of the lettuce and stir to combine.

To prepare the dressing: in a small bowl, combine the mayonnaise, salt, and cayenne pepper.

Pour the dressing over the salad mixture, tossing gently to coat. Arrange the remaining lettuce on a serving dish. Spoon a small portion of the salad mixture onto each ham slice and fold the ham over like a taco.

Mtuzí Wa Samkí

(Kenyan Baked Físh wíth Spícy Sauce)

YIELD: 4 SERVINGS

If plain water was satisfying enough, then the fish would not take the hook.

—Ashanti proverb

4 halibut steaks (2 pounds), 1 inch thick

Sauce:

2 tablespoons vegetable oil
1 large onion, sliced
2 cloves garlic, chopped
1 teaspoon seeded and finely chopped jalapeño pepper
1 16-ounce can tomatoes, diced and the juice discarded
2 tablespoons white cider vinegar
1¼ teaspoons ground cumin
¾ teaspoon ground coriander
½ teaspoon salt

Preheat the oven to 350 degrees.

To prepare the sauce: In a skillet, heat the oil until it is hot but not smoking and sauté the onion, garlic, and jalapeño pepper until the onion is transparent. Stir in the remaining ingredients. Simmer, uncovered, about 5 minutes, stirring occasionally.

Place the halibut steaks in an ungreased oblong baking pan. Spoon the sauce over the fish. Bake uncovered for 25 to 30 minutes. Do not overcook.

Ghana Baked Fish with Tomato Sauce

YIELD: 4 SERVINGS

If the fish in the water grow fat, it is in the interest of the crocodile.

—Ashanti proverb

2 bay leaves
2 black peppercorns
2 cloves garlic, chopped
¼ cup peanut oil plus 1 tablespoon
1 red snapper, whole, about ½ pound of fish per serving
2 tablespoons lemon juice, preferably fresh
1½ medium onions, chopped, about 1 cup
½ teaspoon salt
½ teaspoon cayenne pepper
2 large tomatoes, peeled and chopped
2 teaspoons ketchup
1 teaspoon salt
1 teaspoon black pepper

To prepare the fish: Soak the bay leaves, peppercorns, and garlic in the peanut oil at room temperature for 1 hour.

Preheat the oven to 350 degrees.

Strain the peanut oil and discard the solids. Wash and dry the fish and rub with the seasoned oil, lemon juice, and half the chopped onion. Sprinkle the fish with the salt and cayenne pepper. Bake until the flesh of the fish is opaque at the thickest part (test by inserting the tip of a knife into the thick part), about 50 minutes.

To prepare the tomato sauce: Heat the oil until it is hot but not smoking and sauté the tomatoes and remaining onion until the onion is soft. Add the ketchup, salt, and pepper. Simmer for 10 minutes, stirring frequently. Spoon the sauce over the baked fish.

Camarao à Laurentía
(Mozambíque Shrímp)

YIELD: 4 SERVINGS

When one is at sea, he does not quarrel with the boatman. —Dahomean proverb

12 jumbo shrimp, shelled and deveined, tails left intact
4 tablespoons olive oil
½ cup chopped onion
1 large clove garlic, chopped
1 teaspoon sweet paprika
1 teaspoon ground cumin
⅔ cup canned tomatoes, drained and chopped
2 cups coconut milk
2 tablespoons ground coriander
½ teaspoon salt

Wash the shrimp under cold running water and drain on paper towels. In a heavy skillet, heat 3 tablespoons of the oil until it is hot but not smoking. Add the shrimp and sauté briefly until they are firm and pink, 2 to 3 minutes. Remove the shrimp from the skillet and set aside.

Heat the remaining tablespoon of oil in the skillet and sauté the onion and garlic until translucent but not brown. Stir in the paprika and cumin, then add the tomatoes. Simmer 5 to 8 minutes. Stir in the coconut milk, coriander, and salt. Stir in the shrimp and simmer over low heat for 3 to 4 minutes. Serve over rice.

Ghana Jollof Rice

YIELD: 8 SERVINGS

Although this version of jollof rice hails from Ghana, it is a popular dish in many regions of the African continent. In jollof, the rice is cooked along with the other ingredients, rather than as a separate starch. Jollof contains just about everything you need for a one-dish meal.

2 cups water
1 3-pound chicken, cut into 8 pieces
2 16-ounce cans stewed tomatoes
2 teaspoons salt
¼ teaspoon black pepper
¾ cup cubed, cooked, smoked ham
1 cup uncooked rice
1 large onion, sliced
3 cups shredded green cabbage
½ pound fresh green beans, quartered and stems removed, or 1 10-ounce package frozen or 1 8-ounce can, drained
¼ teaspoon ground cinnamon
¼ teaspoon cayenne pepper

Pour the water into a large pot. Add the chicken, tomatoes, salt, and pepper. Cover, bring to a boil, reduce the heat, and simmer for 30 minutes. Stir in the ham, rice, onion, cabbage, green beans, cinnamon, and cayenne pepper.

Bring to a boil, then reduce heat to low. Cover and simmer until the chicken is fork-tender and the rice is cooked, 25 to 30 minutes.

VEGETABLES

West African Red Beans

YIELD: 6 TO 8 SERVINGS

Here is the forefather of the sassy red bean dish that is so popular in Louisiana.

1 cup dried pinto beans, picked over
1 ¼ cups chopped onion
½ cup peanut or vegetable oil
1 cup canned whole tomatoes, drained and chopped
1 tablespoon tomato paste
1 large clove garlic, minced
¼ teaspoon cayenne pepper
¼ teaspoon white pepper
1 teaspoon salt

Soak the beans overnight in 2 quarts of water, or quick-soak them: put the beans in a heavy pot and cover with 2 quarts of water. Bring to a boil, and boil for 2 to 3 minutes. Remove the pot from the heat and let the beans soak, uncovered, for 1 hour.

Bring the pot of soaked beans to a boil, then reduce the heat to low. Add ¼ cup of the onion and simmer, partly covered, about 1 hour, or until the beans are tender but not mushy. Drain the beans in a large sieve and set them aside.

In a large, heavy skillet, heat the oil until it is hot but not smoking. Sauté the remaining cup of onion until soft and translucent but not brown. Add the tomatoes, tomato paste, garlic, cayenne pepper, white pepper, and salt. Stirring frequently, simmer the mixture until most of the liquid has evaporated. Stir in the beans and cook, uncovered, for 5 to 10 minutes, stirring frequently.

Yataklete Kílkíl
(Ethíopían-Style Vegetables)

YIELD: 8 SERVINGS

Yataklete kilkil is traditionally served as a main course during Lent in Ethiopia. It also makes a tasty side dish.

4 cups water
¼ teaspoon salt
6 small potatoes
3 carrots, scraped and sliced
6 scallions, chopped, including tops
1½ cups fresh green beans, ends removed and cut into 1-inch lengths, or 1 9-ounce package frozen cut green beans
1 tablespoon oil
2 medium onions, thinly sliced
1 green bell pepper, seeded and cut into strips
½ teaspoon chopped jalapeño pepper, ribs and seeds removed
1 clove garlic, chopped
1 teaspoon ground ginger
1 teaspoon salt
½ teaspoon white pepper

In a medium pot, bring the water and salt to a boil. Meanwhile, peel and slice the potatoes. (Drop the potato slices into a bowl of cold water as you prepare them to prevent discoloration.) Drop the potato slices into the boiling water. The water should cover the potatoes. Add the carrots, scallions, and green beans. Bring the vegetables to a rolling boil and cook, uncovered, for 5 minutes. Drain the vegetables in a large colander, then rinse them with cold water. Set them aside in the colander to drain completely.

In a heavy saucepan, heat the oil until it is hot but not smoking. Cook the onions, bell pepper, and jalapeño pepper over low heat until the vegetables are soft but

not brown, about 5 minutes. Add the garlic, ginger, salt, and pepper and stir, then add the potatoes, carrots, scallions, and beans. Stir until the vegetables are coated with the oil mixture. Partly cover the pan and continue cooking about 10 minutes, or until the vegetables are crisp-tender.

Mchícha Wa Nazí
(East Afrícan Spínach)

YIELD: 4 SERVINGS

Coconut milk and peanuts give this spinach dish a wonderful flavor.

2 pounds spinach, washed and stems removed
1 teaspoon salt
2 tablespoons butter
1 cup chopped onion
½ teaspoon chopped fresh hot green chili
1 cup coconut milk
½ cup finely crushed unsalted roasted peanuts

Put the wet spinach leaves and salt in a heavy pot and cover tightly. Steam the spinach over moderate heat until it is tender, about 10 minutes. Drain the spinach in a sieve, chop the leaves coarsely, and set aside.

In a heavy skillet, melt the butter. Add the onion and chili and, stirring frequently, cook until they are soft but not brown. Add the coconut milk and peanuts and simmer over low heat, uncovered, stirring frequently, for 2 to 3 minutes. Add the spinach and cook for 4 or 5 minutes more.

Ugandan Spínach and Símsím

(Spínach and Sesame Seeds)

YIELD: 4 SERVINGS

3 to 4 tablespoons water
½ cup sesame seeds
1 pound fresh spinach, washed, stems removed, and chopped, or 1 10-ounce package frozen chopped spinach, thawed
1 tablespoon butter

Put 3 tablespoons water and the sesame seeds in a heavy saucepan. Stir in the spinach and cover tightly. Bring to a boil, adding another tablespoon of water if necessary. Reduce the heat and simmer until the spinach is tender, 5 to 10 minutes. Drain the spinach in a sieve and return it to the saucepan. Toss with the butter.

Dundu Oníyerí

(West Afrícan Fríed Yams)

YIELD: 6 SERVINGS

Yams are an important ingredient in African cooking. The long, white African yams have a distinctive taste, but they are not usually carried in American grocery stores. Some people in Nigeria believe that eating white yams will make a woman give birth to twins, a sign of luck! I've happily eaten many white yams without any change in the size of my household. Some Asian markets carry a variety of white African yams (cocoyams, wateryams, and white yams) when they are in season; or you can do what my ancestors did when they arrived in America: substitute sweet potatoes.

1 quart water plus 2 tablespoons
½ teaspoon salt
2 pounds yams or sweet potatoes, peeled and cut into ½-inch slices
1 cup flour
1 teaspoon salt
½ teaspoon black pepper
½ teaspoon ground cinnamon
½ teaspoon sweet paprika
2 eggs
¼ cup peanut or vegetable oil

Combine the 1 quart water, salt, and yams or sweet potatoes in a saucepan and bring to a boil. Cook until tender but firm, about 20 minutes. Drain in a colander.

On a plate, combine the flour, salt, pepper, cinnamon, and paprika. In a small bowl, combine the eggs and 2 tablespoons water. Dip the yams into the seasoned flour, then into the egg mixture, and into the flour again. Continue until all the pieces are coated.

In a heavy skillet, heat the oil until it is hot but not smoking. Deep-fry the yams until golden brown. Remove from the pan with a slotted spoon and drain on paper towels.

East African Stuffed Okra

YIELD: 4 SERVINGS

Okra is another African export to America that has become popular across the country.

12 medium okra, washed, tips removed but stems left intact
4 tablespoons lemon juice
2 cloves garlic, minced
2 teaspoons ground turmeric
2 teaspoons curry powder
¼ teaspoon cayenne pepper
1 teaspoon salt
¼ cup vegetable oil

Cut the washed okra lengthwise, leaving the stem end intact so that the 2 halves remain connected. In a small bowl, combine the lemon juice with the garlic. Add the turmeric, curry powder, cayenne pepper, and salt. Stir until the mixture forms a thick paste. Spread the paste on the cut sides of the okra and press the sides together firmly.

In a skillet, heat the oil until it is hot but not smoking and fry the okra until lightly browned.

Rice Foofoo

YIELD: 4 SERVINGS

Foofoo (also known as fufu, foufou, pap, and putu) is the starchy accompaniment to many main dishes in Africa. For generations African women have pounded dried yams, cassava slices, corn kernels, plantain, or rice into flour to make foofoo. Foofoo has the consistency of a dumpling and is shaped into a ball. Small pieces of foofoo are pinched off, dipped into a soup or stew, and popped into the mouth. The way some Africans use foofoo to scoop up their food is practically an art. This is a simpler version of the flour-based foofoo recipes, but it is comparable in taste and texture.

2½ cups water
1 teaspoon salt
1 cup rice

In a medium pot, boil the water. Add the salt and rice. Cook the rice over moderate heat until it is mushy, adding more water as needed, 10 to 15 minutes. Drain in a colander and return the rice to the pot. With a wooden spoon, press the rice against the sides of the pot until it is smooth and stiff. Scrape into a bowl. Wet your hands and shape the rice into 4 balls.

VARIATIONS:

To make yam foofoo, boil 2 cups water and add 2 teaspoons salt. Peel and dice 3 to 4 medium yams and boil them in the water until tender. Drain in a colander. Mash the yams with a potato masher or fork until smooth. Shape into balls.

Yebaqela Kík We't

(Ethíopían Fava Beans)

YIELD: 6 SERVINGS

Fava beans are large legumes also known as horse beans and broad beans. Fava beans are a pale green color when fresh, reddish-brown when dried, and have a nutty taste. Fava beans date to ancient times. They were often the main food given to the African captives during the "middle passage," the journey from Africa to America.

2 cups fresh fava beans, washed
6 cups water
1½ cups vegetable oil
2 cups chopped red onion
1 tablespoon minced garlic
1 teaspoon cayenne pepper
¼ teaspoon ground cumin
1 teaspoon salt

Put the beans in a large pot and cover with the water. Boil until the beans are tender but not mushy (anywhere from 5 to 15 minutes, depending on the freshness of the beans).

In a skillet, heat the oil until it is hot but not smoking and sauté the onion and garlic. Add the cayenne, cumin, and salt. Cook until the onion has softened, about 5 minutes, stirring occasionally.

Add the onion and garlic mixture to the beans and bring to a boil. Reduce the heat and simmer for 30 minutes.

BREADS AND DESSERTS

Ethiopian Injera Bread

YIELD: 6 SERVINGS

Injera is a must for most Ethiopian meals. This pancake-like bread is used as a "plate"; each dish in an evening's meal is served on the injera. The proper way to eat most Ethiopian dishes is to scoop up the meat or vegetables with a piece of injera and pop it into your mouth.

Injera is traditionally made from teff, a highly nutritious cereal grain, similar to rye, which the Ethiopians also call lovegrass. Teff is ground into a flour and mixed with water to make the fermented batter-like dough used for injera. This is an easier version of the authentic recipe for injera. It takes some practice to get it perfect; don't get discouraged!

5 tablespoons all-purpose flour
3 cups Aunt Jemima's Deluxe Easy Pour Pancake Mix
¼ teaspoon baking soda
3½ cups club soda at room temperature
1½ cups water

In a deep mixing bowl, combine the flour, pancake mix, and baking soda. Stirring constantly with a whisk or spoon, slowly pour in the club soda and water. Continue stirring until the mixture is smooth. Strain the batter by pressing it through a fine sieve set over a bowl. The batter will be thin.

Cook the injera as you would cook a pancake; use a griddle, a 10-inch skillet, or an omelet pan. Warm the griddle or ungreased pan over moderate heat until it is just hot enough to set the batter without browning it. To test the heat, pour 1 tablespoon of the batter into the center of the pan. The bottom surface should solidify immediately without becoming brown.

Remove the pan from the heat. Pour in about ¼ cup of batter. Tilt the pan so

that the batter coats the bottom evenly. Partly cover the pan and cook the bread over moderate heat until the top is spongy, moist, and dotted with tiny air holes, about 1 minute. Check the bottom of the injera periodically. Do not let it brown or let the edges become too crisp. The bottom should be smooth, dry, and somewhat shiny.

When the injera is done, remove the pan from the heat. Place the injera on a platter or in a large, flat basket. Repeat the procedure until all the batter has been cooked. Allow one injera to drape over the edge of the platter or basket. Fold the rest of the injera into quarters and arrange them in a fan in the center. Serve immediately.

Tanzanian Baked Bananas

YIELD: 8 SERVINGS

Sweets and desserts are not a large part of the African diet. For many years, sugar was extremely expensive in Africa, and sugary dishes were reserved for a treat during the Christmas holidays. This recipe from Tanzania makes an easy-to-prepare, healthful, and delicious dessert.

4 large, ripe, unpeeled bananas
2 tablespoons melted butter
3 tablespoons packed brown sugar
1 teaspoon lemon juice

Preheat the oven to 425 degrees.

Cut off the ends of the bananas. Place the unpeeled bananas on an ungreased cookie sheet or in a baking pan. Bake for 15 minutes, or until the skins burst and turn black. Discard the skins and cut the bananas lengthwise. Mix the butter, brown sugar, and lemon and drizzle over the cooked bananas.

East African Sweet Potato Pudding

YIELD: 8 SERVINGS

I believe this wonderful pudding traveled to America and gradually became the filling for our sweet potato pie.

1 quart water
6 medium sweet potatoes (about 2 pounds), peeled and cut into ½-inch cubes
3 cups milk
1 cup heavy cream
½ cup sugar
½ teaspoon ground saffron
½ teaspoon ground cardamom

In a heavy saucepan, boil the water. Drop in the sweet potatoes. Cook the potatoes, uncovered, until tender, 25 to 30 minutes. Drain the potatoes in a sieve or colander and return them to the pan. Add the milk, cream, sugar, saffron, and cardamom. Stirring frequently with a wooden spoon, bring the mixture to a boil over moderate heat. Reduce the heat to low and simmer, uncovered, about 1 hour, stirring often. The pudding is done when it is smooth and is thick enough to hold its shape almost solidly in the spoon.

With the back of the spoon, rub the pudding through a fine sieve into a serving bowl. Refrigerate the pudding until cool. Before serving, sprinkle the top with a little additional ground cardamom.

DRINKS

Moroccan Almond Milk

YIELD: 4 SERVINGS

This soothing drink is wonderful whether you serve it after dinner, along with or instead of coffee, or before bedtime.

1½ cups roasted almonds, ground fine
½ cup packed brown sugar
1 cup water
2 cups milk
1 tablespoon orange zest

In a bowl, combine the almonds and sugar. Stir in ½ cup of the water and set the mixture aside for 30 minutes. Pour the mixture into a blender and blend on low speed. With the blender running, slowly add the remaining ½ cup of water and blend until smooth. Set the mixture aside for another 30 minutes. In a saucepan, warm the milk; do not boil it. Add the orange zest. Stir the almond mixture into the milk and mix well.

African Fruit Punch

YIELD: 8 TO 10 SERVINGS

2½ cups lemonade
1 cup orange juice
1 cup pineapple juice
1 cup papaya juice (available in African and Caribbean markets)
1 cup guava juice (available in African and Carribbean markets)

Mix all the juices together in a pitcher and chill. Serve over ice.

Chinanadzi
(Pineapple Drink)

YIELD: 8 TO 10 SERVINGS

1 large ripe pineapple
1 teaspoon ground ginger
1 teaspoon ground cloves
2 tablespoons sugar
5 cups boiling water

Peel and slice the pineapple and place it in a large bowl. Add the spices and sugar. Pour the boiling water over the ingredients. Cover the bowl and refrigerate overnight. Strain the drink into a pitcher. Serve over ice.

THE PEPPER POT IS NEVER EMPTY

The Caribbean

From many people, one people.
—West Indian proverb

Caribbean culture is like a pepper pot, a fantastic tradition that is an Island treasure. A pepper pot is not only a cooking vessel, but also a spicy stew made of whatever meats or vegetables the cook has at hand. Peppers and the juice of a cassava root are added to the pot. Small serving portions are removed from the pot and new ingredients added, so the pepper pot is never empty and never quite full. Years of simmering and blending give the ingredients of the pepper pot an unmatched flavor. Some pepper pots are considered so valuable that they are willed from one generation to the next.

The Islands were originally populated by the Arawak and the Carib Indians and colonized in the sixteenth and seventeenth centuries by the French, Spanish, and English. African slaves were brought to the Islands in large numbers. By the second half of the seventeenth century, the slaves outnumbered their masters. The complexion of the Islands, as well as the cuisine, began to change.

The slaves labored in the sugarcane fields, and in their masters' kitchens. They were chosen for their occupations based on their strength and temperament. The Spanish colonists picked their slaves from the Yorubas of Nigeria, in West Africa. The English preferred the Ashanti from the Gold Coast. The French purchased Dahomeans, Congolese, and Ibos to do their field work, and the mild-mannered Mandingoes for house servants.

The races intermingled, resulting in a new population of fair-skinned people called Creoles. The Creole language and cuisine are now as much a part of the Islands as palm trees and beaches.

The tastes and techniques of the French, Spanish, and English colonists influenced many of the recipes you will find in this section. You will also find here the curries and spices that were introduced by slaves brought from India.

The African influence on Caribbean cooking is evident in the preparation of jerk barbecue and the use of peppers. The African slave cooks also created new recipes by combining the fruits and vegetables they transplanted from Africa with foods that were common to the Caribbean.

The melding of ancient African spices and cooking techniques with traditional European fare produced a range of Caribbean dishes whose flavors are virtually unmatched in other parts of the world.

A MARINADE AND A SAUCE

Caribbean Marinade

YIELD: ¾ CUP

Caribbean cooks use this basic seasoning combination along with their own favorite herbs and spices. That's why no dish tastes exactly the same from place to place. This marinade was used as early as the sixteenth century to preserve and tenderize tough cuts of meat. It adds a wonderful flavor to roasted, stewed, or braised meats. It is very similar to the combination of herbs and spices used by African cooks and is probably a variation of a slave recipe. This is enough marinade for about 3 pounds of meat. It's delicious mixed with hamburger meat, added to stews, or used as a marinade for pork, chicken, or fish.

1 medium onion, grated
1 clove garlic, minced
1 scallion, chopped
½ cup chopped celery leaves
2 tablespoons malt vinegar
2 tablespoons cooking sherry
1 tablespoon soy sauce
1 teaspoon cayenne pepper

Combine all the ingredients.

This marinade can be rubbed into any type of meat. Let the meat stand at room temperature for 1 hour, turning frequently, before baking, braising, or barbecuing.

To make a sauce or gravy for baked or braised meats, scrape the remaining marinade from the surface of the cooked meat. Combine the cooked marinade with any juices that have collected in the bottom of the baking pan. These ingredients can be used as a sauce, or thicken them with a little flour and water as needed to make gravy.

Salsa Roja Para Frijoles Negros
(Sweet Pepper Sauce for Black Beans)

YIELD: ABOUT 4 CUPS

This salsa is a great way to spice up a bowl of black beans.

1 cup olive oil
1½ cups peeled and chopped tomatoes
2 cloves garlic, minced
¼ teaspoon black pepper
½ teaspoon cayenne pepper
¼ teaspoon dried oregano
½ teaspoon sugar
Salt to taste
½ cup tomato puree
2 cups pimentos, drained and chopped, liquid reserved
¼ cup white vinegar

In a saucepan, heat the oil until it is hot but not smoking and add the tomatoes. Stir with a wooden spoon about 5 minutes, or until they are cooked to a soft pulp. Add the remaining ingredients except the vinegar and simmer over low heat, stirring occasionally. When the sauce has thickened, remove the pan from the heat and stir in the vinegar.

SALADS AND SNACKS

Rice Salad

YIELD: 4 TO 6 SERVINGS

This salad was created out of a recipe used by slave cooks from Malaysia. It's so colorful that it looks like it's all dressed up for a Jamaican jamboree.

⅓ cup plain low-fat yogurt
1 tablespoon raisins
1 tablespoon minced onion
1 teaspoon curry powder
⅛ teaspoon salt
⅛ teaspoon black pepper
⅛ teaspoon ground turmeric
2 teaspoons cider vinegar
1 cup white rice, cooked and cooled
¼ cup coarsely chopped green bell pepper
¼ cup coarsely chopped red bell pepper
Lettuce leaves

In a medium bowl, blend the yogurt, raisins, onion, curry powder, salt, pepper, turmeric, and vinegar. Stir in the cold rice and bell peppers. Refrigerate. Serve on a bed of lettuce leaves.

Shrimp Salad with Coconut Cream

YIELD: 8 SERVINGS

No Caribbean dinner would be complete without a dish containing coconut or shellfish. This salad combines both, with appetizing results.

1 cup milk
1 cup grated unsweetened coconut, fresh or packaged
1 tablespoon vegetable oil
2 green bell peppers, seeded and chopped
2 shallots, minced
1 tablespoon chopped peanuts
2 tablespoons soy sauce
1 teaspoon salt
2 pounds medium shrimp, cooked and shelled

In a saucepan, combine the milk and coconut and bring the mixture to a boil. Remove from the heat immediately and set aside for 30 minutes. Press the mixture through a sieve to extract the cream. Discard the pulp.

In a skillet, heat the oil until it is hot but not smoking and sauté the peppers and shallots. Remove from the heat and add the peanuts, soy sauce, and salt. Stir in the cream from the coconut. Arrange the shrimp on a platter and pour the dressing over them. Chill and serve.

Green Papaya Salad

YIELD: 4 SERVINGS

Papaya or pawpaw is a South American import to the Islands. Although papayas are fairly bland, when mixed with other fruits, vegetables, or spices they enhance the flavor of a dish. Green papaya tastes a little like summer squash and is often used as a vegetable of sorts, as it is in this salad.

2 large green papayas, peeled, seeded, and diced (about 2 cups)
¼ teaspoon salt
½ teaspoon dry mustard
1 teaspoon chopped parsley
1 teaspoon lime juice
¼ teaspoon salt
⅛ teaspoon black pepper
3 hard-cooked eggs, chopped
2 whole red pimentos, drained and chopped
1½ tablespoons mayonnaise
4 crisp lettuce leaves

Place the papaya and salt in a small saucepan. Cover with water and simmer until the papaya is tender, about 20 minutes. Drain and refrigerate. In a bowl, combine the mustard, parsley, lime juice, salt, pepper, eggs, pimento, and mayonnaise, then add the papaya and mix well. Serve the salad on a bed of lettuce leaves.

Fruited Cabbage

YIELD: 6 SERVINGS

Fruit and cabbage are an unusual combination, but a tasty one when prepared this way.

1½ pounds cabbage, shredded
¼ cup raisins
1 cup diced pineapple
2 medium onions, diced
1 cup water
Juice of 1 lime
⅛ teaspoon salt

In a medium saucepan, combine the cabbage with the fruit and onions. Add the water, lime juice, and salt, and bring to a boil. Simmer about 40 minutes, or until the liquid has evaporated and the cabbage is tender.

Límbo Cakes

YIELD: 6 SERVINGS

It's much easier to make these puffy, crisp snacks than it is to do the acrobatic dance they are named for.

3 or 4 large green plantains, peeled and sliced into 2-inch rounds
4 cups salted water
2 cups vegetable oil
Salt to taste

Soak the plantain slices in the salted water about 30 minutes to remove some of the starch. Drain the slices and pat dry with paper towels. In a deep, heavy saucepan, heat the oil until it is hot but not smoking, add the plantains, and cook about 5 minutes. Do not brown. Turn the plantains once. Drain on paper towels.

One by one, place the plantain slices on a sheet of waxed paper, cover with another sheet, and use a rolling pin or the flat side of a mallet to flatten to ½ inch thickness. Return the plantains to the hot oil and fry until crisp and brown. Drain on paper towels and sprinkle with salt.

Meat Patties Wrapped in Pastry

YIELD: 12 PATTIES

Annatto (achiote) seeds are rust-red dried seeds that give cooking oil or lard a bright orange-yellow color and a delicate flavor. They can be found in some grocery stores and most Latino markets. In this recipe, the seeds must be removed from the hot oil as soon as it takes on the orange-yellow tint. Do not overcook. You can also find annatto or achiote oil in some markets, and you can use this in place of the seeds. You can also substitute saffron or turmeric.

Filling:

2 tablespoons vegetable oil
1 teaspoon annatto seeds (or substitute 1 teaspoon ground saffron or turmeric)
1 pound lean ground beef
1 medium onion, finely chopped
1 clove garlic, minced
1 cup peeled, seeded, and chopped tomato
½ teaspoon salt
½ teaspoon black pepper
¼ teaspoon cayenne pepper
½ teaspoon dried thyme
2 eggs, lightly beaten

Pastry:

2½ cups all-purpose flour
⅛ teaspoon salt
¾ cup (1½ sticks) cold unsalted butter
⅓ cup ice water
1 egg white, beaten until foamy

To prepare the filling: In a large frying pan, heat the oil until it is hot but not smoking and add the annatto seeds, saffron, or turmeric. Cook over moderate heat until the oil is orange-yellow, about 2 minutes. If using annatto seeds, remove them with a slotted spoon and discard.

Add the beef, breaking it up with a fork as it cooks, until it begins to brown. Add the onion and garlic and cook until the onion is soft. Add the tomato, salt, black pepper, cayenne pepper, and thyme. Cook, stirring, for 5 minutes or longer, until the mixture is quite dry. Remove from the heat and stir in the eggs. Return to the heat and cook, stirring, for 2 or 3 minutes longer. Cool to room temperature.

To prepare the pastry: Mix the flour and salt with a pastry blender or fork, or in the bowl of a food processor. Add the butter 1 tablespoon at a time, cutting it into the flour thoroughly. When all the butter has been added, the flour mixture should be grainy like cornmeal. Slowly add the ice water to the flour, about 3 tablespoons at a time, using your hands or the processor to mix it after each addition until the dough forms a ball. Divide the dough in half and pat each half into a disk about ½ inch thick. Wrap the disks in plastic wrap and refrigerate for at least 30 minutes.

To assemble the patties: Preheat the oven to 425 degrees.

Flour a work surface and rolling pin and roll out half the dough until it is a strip about 8 inches wide and ⅛ inch thick. Using a floured coffee cup or biscuit cutter, cut each half of the pastry into 6 circles. Place ½ cup of the meat mixture on one side of each circle and fold it over into a crescent. Seal the edges by pinching with your fingers or crimping with a fork. Brush with the beaten egg white and prick the tops to let steam escape. Repeat with the remaining dough. Bake on an ungreased cookie sheet for 20 to 30 minutes, or until lightly browned.

Codfish Cakes
(Stamp and Go)

YIELD: 24 CAKES

Stamp and go, or codfish cakes, are popular snacks and appetizers in Jamaica. The dish is so named because you can buy it from one of the food vendors that populate Jamaican bus stops and jump on the next bus.

½ pound salt codfish
1 cup all-purpose flour
1 teaspoon baking powder
½ teaspoon salt
1 egg, lightly beaten
¾ cup milk
1 tablespoon butter, melted
1 tablespoon sweet paprika
1 medium onion, minced
½ teaspoon cayenne pepper
Vegetable oil or lard for deep-frying

Put the codfish in a bowl and fill the bowl with warm water. Soak the fish for 2 to 3 hours to remove the salt. Drain and rinse the fish in cool water, place in a saucepan, and cover with boiling water. Simmer until the fish is tender, about 15 minutes. Drain, remove the bones and skin, and shred the fish.

Sift together the flour, baking powder, and salt. In a small bowl, combine the egg, milk, butter, and paprika, and stir into the dry ingredients. Add the fish, onion, and pepper and mix well.

In a deep skillet or deep-fryer, heat the oil until it is hot but not smoking. Drop tablespoonfuls of the fish in mixture into the hot oil and fry until golden brown. Drain on paper towels and serve hot.

SOUPS

Cucumber and Shrimp Soup

YIELD: 6 SERVINGS

If it's too hot to cook, this refreshing soup offers the perfect solution—it's cool, it's nutritious, and if you buy precooked shrimp it can be prepared without using any heat.

3 cups plain low-fat yogurt
1¼ cups sour cream
Juice of 1 lemon
1 large cucumber
1 cup diced cooked shrimp
¼ teaspoon minced fresh dill
½ teaspoon salt
½ teaspoon black pepper
¼ teaspoon garlic powder
½ teaspoon Worcestershire sauce

In a medium bowl, combine well the yogurt, sour cream, and lemon juice. Add the remaining ingredients, cover, and refrigerate for at least 1 hour before serving.

Breadfruit Soup

YIELD: 8 SERVINGS

Captain Bligh of the Bounty *introduced breadfruit trees to the tropics in 1792. Despite its name, breadfruit is a vegetable, with a starchy potato-like taste and a brown seed that looks like a chestnut. Ripe breadfruit are only edible when cooked. If fresh breadfruit is not available, you can use the canned variety, or white yams or potatoes. This soup tastes good hot or cold.*

1 breadfruit, peeled and cut into small pieces, or 1 14- to 16-ounce can, drained (available in Asian markets)
3 cups water
3 cloves garlic, minced
½ teaspoon salt
½ teaspoon black pepper
6 chicken or beef bouillon cubes
1 medium onion, chopped
1½ cups heavy cream

Place the breadfruit, water, garlic, salt, pepper, bouillon cubes, and onion in a large pot. Bring the ingredients to a boil, reduce the heat to moderate, and stir until the soup is slightly thickened. With the back of a spoon or a potato masher, mash the breadfruit. Strain the soup, mashing any lumps through a sieve. Return the soup to the pot and add the cream. Simmer over low heat, stirring frequently, for 10 minutes.

SEAFOOD

Grilled Fish with Spicy Marinade

YIELD: 6 SERVINGS

A fish trap doesn't make any noise, but it does good work. —Slave proverb

1 teaspoon dried tarragon
1 teaspoon dried basil
1 teaspoon dried thyme
1 teaspoon hot paprika
1 teaspoon dried oregano
1 teaspoon fennel seed
1 teaspoon aniseed
2 tablespoons lemon juice
2 tablespoons lime juice
1 tablespoon white-wine vinegar
2 tablespoons Worcestershire sauce
½ Scotch bonnet or jalapeño pepper, minced
2 cups vegetable oil
6 fillets mild, light-fleshed fish such as flounder, bass, or catfish

In a shallow bowl, combine all the ingredients except the fish. Add the fish and coat each piece thoroughly with the marinade. Refrigerate for at least 1 hour.

Remove the rack from the grill and oil it with vegetable oil. Allow the coals to become partly white with ash before cooking the fish. Place the marinated fish on the grill, turning once when the flesh becomes opaque. Do not overcook.

Caribbean Stuffed Red Snapper

YIELD: 6 TO 8 SERVINGS

When you purchase the whole red snapper for this recipe, ask to have it scaled with tail, fins, and head intact but with the backbone removed. The fish is filled from fin to fin with a flavorful herb stuffing and then coated with bread crumbs. It's fabulous!

1 3- to 4-pound whole red snapper
1 lime, quartered
Salt for rubbing the fish

Stuffing:

2 cups bread crumbs
½ cup (1 stick) butter, melted
4 tablespoons chopped chives
4 tablespoons chopped parsley
¼ to ½ teaspoon cayenne pepper
1 small onion, grated
Zest and juice of 1 small lime
1 teaspoon salt
1 teaspoon white pepper
1 teaspoon dried thyme
1 teaspoon dried sweet marjoram

Coating:

2 egg whites
1 cup bread crumbs

Wash the fish and rub inside and out with the quartered lime and salt. Refrigerate for at least 10 minutes. Wipe off the lime juice and salt.

Preheat the oven to 300 degrees.

Combine all the stuffing ingredients and fill the cavity of the snapper.

With a whisk, beat the egg white until fluffy. Coat the fish by rubbing on the egg white and sprinkling on the bread crumbs.

Bake the fish until the flesh is opaque, allowing about 10 minutes to the pound. Do not overcook.

Swordfish with Tomatillo Sauce

YIELD: 4 SERVINGS

Tomatillos look like green, husk-covered tomatoes. You can find them fresh or canned in many supermarkets. They make a wonderful sauce for baked or broiled fish, and this tomatillo sauce can also be used as a dip.

4 swordfish steaks, about ¾ inch thick (about 2 pounds)
2 tablespoons lemon juice

Tomatillo Sauce:

½ pound fresh tomatillos, husks removed and quartered, or 1 11-ounce can tomatillos, drained and quartered
1 large tomato, chopped
½ cup chopped cilantro
½ small red bell pepper, seeded and chopped
½ cup white vinegar
1 teaspoon salt
½ Scotch bonnet pepper, forced through a garlic press

Sprinkle the swordfish with the lemon juice, cover, and set aside. To prepare the sauce, grind all the ingredients except the Scotch bonnet pepper in a blender or food processor until fine. The sauce should be dry and some solids should remain in it. If it is too mushy, add a little more vinegar. Mix in half of the crushed Scotch bonnet pepper. This pepper is very hot, and it takes about 15 minutes for its flavor to seep through the other ingredients. It is best to wait for 15 minutes and taste the sauce again before adding any additional pepper.

Grill or broil the swordfish 3 minutes per side, or until it is still slightly pink in the center. If you are grilling the fish, remove the rack from the grill and oil it with vegetable oil. Allow the coals to become partly white with ash before cooking the fish.

Sprinkle the fish with salt and pepper and serve immediately with the tomatillo sauce.

Fish Poached in Court Bouillon

YIELD: 6 SERVINGS

This is a relaxed Caribbean court bouillon, not the fancier French version. Poach the fish 10 minutes per 1 inch of thickness. Do not test by flaking, since by then the fish is already too dry.

2 cups cold water
7 tablespoons lime juice
1 carrot, cut into ½-inch slices
1 medium onion, sliced
1 stalk celery, diced
1 whole fresh Anaheim pepper
2 whole cloves
3 sprigs parsley
2 bay leaves
1 teaspoon salt
1 teaspoon black pepper
¼ teaspoon dried thyme
2 pounds fish (bass, catfish, cod, orange roughy, salmon, tuna, sole, trout, or flounder), cut into 1-inch-thick fillets

Put all the ingredients except the fish in a large saucepan. Bring to a boil and simmer, uncovered, for 30 minutes. Strain the court bouillon, reserving the vegetables in a separate bowl and discarding the cloves, bay leaves, and hot pepper. Refrigerate the liquid until cool.

Pour the cool court bouillon back into the saucepan and heat to a simmer. Put the fresh fillets in the court bouillon, cover, and simmer gently about 10 minutes. Using a slotted spatula, remove the fish to a platter. Add the reserved vegetables to the remaining court bouillon and serve it as a sauce.

Crawfish Angelique

YIELD: 4 SERVINGS

You better not shake hands with a crawfish. —Slave proverb

4 slices bacon, diced
1 large onion, diced
2 stalks celery, diced
1 large green bell pepper, seeded and diced
1 clove garlic, minced
1 12-ounce can tomato juice
1 14-ounce can whole tomatoes with liquid
1 teaspoon Worcestershire sauce
2 cups water
2 bay leaves
1 teaspoon salt
¼ teaspoon black pepper
⅛ teaspoon cayenne pepper
12 crawfish tails, cooked, meat removed and cubed

In a large pot, cook the bacon until browned and crisp. Using a slotted spoon, remove the bacon and drain on paper towels.

Sauté the onion, celery, pepper, and garlic in the bacon fat until the vegetables are soft. Add the tomato juice, tomatoes, Worcestershire sauce, water, bay leaves, salt, and the black and cayenne pepper. Simmer for 15 to 20 minutes.

Add the crawfish and bacon and cook for 10 minutes longer. Remove the bay leaves. Serve over rice.

Papaya Shrimp with Sautéed Garlic

YIELD: 4 SERVINGS

This creamy dish has a delightful flavor and looks elegant when served on pretty china and decorated with the seasoned papaya strips.

½ cup (1 stick) butter or margarine
2 cloves garlic, minced
1 stalk celery, diced
1 medium onion, diced
½ cup water
½ cup white-wine vinegar
2 tablespoons sugar
1 bay leaf
4 cups fish stock or chicken broth
2 cups heavy cream
24 large shrimp, shelled and deveined
½ teaspoon salt
½ teaspoon black pepper
2 small, ripe papayas, peeled, seeded, and cut into strips
¼ teaspoon dried thyme
¼ teaspoon dried basil

In a large saucepan over low heat, melt 4 tablespoons of the butter or margarine. Add the garlic and sauté until lightly browned, about 10 minutes. Add the celery and onion and cook until the onion is soft and transparent. Add the water, vinegar, sugar, bay leaf, and stock or broth. Increase the heat to high and cook until the liquid is reduced by half. Stir in the cream.

In a skillet, melt the remaining butter or margarine. Add the shrimp and cook until slightly pink, 2 or 3 minutes. Add the salt and pepper.

In a medium bowl, toss the papaya strips with the basil and thyme.

Spoon the sauce onto 4 dinner plates, set strips of papaya in the center of each, and surround with 6 cooked shrimp per serving.

MEATS

Chicken with Coconut Sauce

YIELD: 4 SERVINGS

When the preacher comes by for Sunday dinner, it makes the chickens cry.

—Slave proverb

All-purpose flour for dredging
1 teaspoon salt
1 teaspoon black pepper
¼ teaspoon sweet paprika
1 chicken, about 2½ pounds, quartered
¼ cup vegetable oil
1 medium onion, sliced
1 green bell pepper, seeded and sliced
1 medium tomato, peeled and sliced
½ teaspoon curry powder
¼ teaspoon ground saffron
1½ cups chicken broth
3 tablespoons unsweetened grated coconut

In a large brown paper bag, combine the flour, salt, pepper, and paprika. Drop in the chicken pieces and shake until well coated.

In a heavy skillet, heat the oil until it is hot but not smoking. Add the onion, bell pepper, and tomato and cook over low heat until the vegetables are wilted and tender, about 8 minutes. Remove the vegetables from the skillet with a slotted spoon and set aside.

Add the chicken to the skillet and sprinkle it with the curry powder and saffron.

Cook for 15 minutes over low heat, turning occasionally, until lightly browned. Return the vegetables to the skillet, cover, and continue cooking over low heat until the chicken is tender, about 20 minutes.

While the chicken is cooking, heat the broth in a small saucepan. Add the coconut and simmer about 10 minutes. Strain into a small bowl, then pour the liquid over the chicken. Stir well. Cover and continue to simmer the chicken and vegetables until the seasonings are well blended, about 10 minutes.

Duck with Banana Stuffing

YIELD: 4 SERVINGS

When in Rome . . . use what's available. This innovative stuffing blends ingredients that are plentiful on the Islands and in America, with delicious results.

1 3- to 4-pound duck
1 tablespoon lime or lemon juice
1½ teaspoons salt

Stuffing:

2 ripe bananas, mashed
1 tablespoon lemon zest
½ teaspoon salt
¼ teaspoon Tabasco sauce
⅛ teaspoon ground nutmeg
⅛ teaspoon ground cinnamon
⅛ teaspoon ground cloves
1½ cups packaged croutons

Preheat the oven to 350 degrees.

Rinse the duck inside and out and pat dry. Rub the body cavity with the lime or lemon juice. Rub the salt over the skin of the duck, then prick the skin with a sharp fork to allow the fat to drain. Set aside.

Combine all the stuffing ingredients and fill the body cavity of the duck. Any left-over stuffing can be baked in a separate pan while you bake the duck. Place the duck, breast side up, on a rack in an uncovered, shallow pan and bake, basting occasionally with the pan drippings, until done, 2 to 2½ hours.

Gríots

YIELD: 4 SERVINGS

African storytellers and historians are called griots. I don't know how this dish got its name, but I like to think it might have been served as a reward for a wonderful evening of stories. These flavorful cubes of pork are popular treats in Haiti and are often served with mashed plantains, sliced avocados, and watercress.

1 cup chopped onion
¼ cup chopped shallots or chives
1 cup orange juice
¼ cup lime juice
¼ cup water
⅛ teaspoon dried thyme
½ teaspoon salt
½ teaspoon black pepper
2 tablespoons vegetable oil
2 pounds boneless pork, cut into 2-inch cubes

Put all the ingredients except the pork in a bowl and mix well. Add the pork and toss until well coated. Marinate in the refrigerator for at least 4 hours. Drain off the marinade and set it aside.

In a frying pan, heat the oil until it is hot but not smoking and brown the pork on all sides. Add the marinade and cover. Simmer over low heat for 30 minutes. Uncover and increase the heat to moderate. Cook until the liquids have evaporated, 8 to 10 minutes.

Spícy Island Spareríbs

YIELD: 4 SERVINGS

This is one of my favorite ways to prepare pork ribs in the oven. The brown sugar, vinegar, soy sauce, and pineapple give the meat a tangy, delicious taste, and the ginger and hot sauce add just the right touch of spiciness. Frequent basting keeps the meat moist and tender.

1 2-pound pork rib slab
¾ cup packed brown sugar
¼ cup white vinegar
2 tablespoons soy sauce
1 teaspoon salt
½ teaspoon ground ginger
1 14-ounce can crushed pineapple with juice
¼ cup shredded unsweetened coconut (optional)
½ teaspoon Tabasco sauce

Cut the slab into individual ribs and put the pieces in a large pot. Cover the ribs with water and simmer for 20 minutes. Drain off the water and put the ribs in a baking pan. In a small saucepan, combine the brown sugar, vinegar, soy sauce, salt, and ginger. Bring to a boil. Add the pineapple with juice and the coconut, if desired. Reduce the heat and simmer the mixture for 5 minutes. Remove from the heat and stir in the Tabasco sauce. You may want to add more brown sugar if you like a sweeter sauce, or more Tabasco sauce if you prefer a spicier version.

Brush each rib with the sauce. Heat the broiler and broil about 10 minutes on each side or until done, basting often.

Jerk Pork

YIELD: 8 SERVINGS

Jerk is the Caribbean method of marinating meats before barbecuing. The technique for making jerk was created by the Arawaks, the first settlers of the Caribbean Islands, and developed into a mouthwatering Island tradition by the Maroons, runaway slaves whose guerrilla tactics against Caribbean slaveowners eventually won them their freedom. The combined methods of spicing and smoking the meat preserved it in the remote places where the Maroons took refuge. The vegetables and spices used in jerk can easily be found in the wild on the Islands and in our own tamer grocery stores. Jerk is one of the most popular dishes in Jamaica, and jerk "cook shacks" dot the Islands like palm trees.

4 tablespoons ground allspice
7 scallions, chopped
½ Scotch bonnet or jalapeño pepper
2 cloves garlic
4 sprigs fresh thyme or 1 tablespoon dried
5 bay leaves
1 teaspoon salt
1 teaspoon black pepper
5 pounds thick-cut pork loin chops

Place all the ingredients except the pork in a blender or food processor. Grind the spices to a paste, adding 1 tablespoon vegetable oil if necessary. Rinse the pork, pat dry, and put it in a pan. Coat it with the jerk paste. Cover the pan with plastic wrap, refrigerate, and marinate for at least 1 hour. Jerk is best when it has marinated overnight in the refrigerator.

Make a fire in the grill and allow the coals to become partly white with ash before cooking the pork. If desired, place sprigs of thyme or bay leaves on the coals for added flavor. Place the marinated meat on the grill. Cook about 10 minutes, turning once. Cook until done, about another 20 minutes.

Puerto Rícan Píñon

YIELD: 6 SERVINGS

This is a great dish for breakfast or brunch. It will taste even better if you have an audience to watch you prepare it. The trick is to flip the egg and meat mixture out of the pan onto a curved pot lid. Then you slide the piñon back into the pan again on top of another layer of eggs. It sounds (and looks) harder than it is. Who knows, your guests may be so impressed they'll even volunteer to do the dishes!

1 pound pork sausage or chorizo, crumbled
4 ripe plantains (skin should be almost black), peeled and sliced lengthwise
6 eggs
½ tablespoon prepared salsa
½ teaspoon salt
½ teaspoon black pepper
3 tablespoons vegetable oil

In a skillet, fry the sausage or chorizo until brown. Remove the meat from the skillet with a slotted spoon. Fry the plantains in the oil remaining in the pan until golden brown. Remove the fried plantains.

In a bowl, beat together the eggs, salsa, salt, and pepper. In a clean skillet, heat the oil until it is hot but not smoking. Pour half the egg mixture into the pan. Do not stir. Working quickly, layer half the plantain slices over the eggs, spread the meat over the plantain, and top with the remaining plantain slices. Cook over moderate heat until the eggs are firm, about 3 minutes.

Take a pot lid and invert the contents onto the underside of the lid. Add enough oil to the pan to cook the remaining egg mixture and pour it into the pan. Slide the piñon back off the pot lid into the pan on top of the raw eggs (the cooked eggs remain on top). Cook until the eggs on the bottom are done, about 3 minutes.

Papaya Beef

YIELD: 6 SERVINGS

This recipe has been used since the times of slavery. Most of the meat on a plantation went to the owners; slaves seldom ate meat, and when they did, it was usually the toughest cuts. Innovative slave cooks found a way to tenderize the meat by using slices of papaya, which contains the enzyme papain, a natural tenderizer.

1 cup lentils
1 large papaya, peeled and sliced, seeds removed and retained
3 pounds round steak, cut into 6 steaks
1 tablespoon olive oil
1 medium yellow onion, sliced
1 teaspoon salt
1 teaspoon black pepper
1 tablespoon Worcestershire sauce
1 large tomato, peeled and chopped

In a medium pot, cover the lentils with water, and simmer for 30 to 40 minutes, or until tender. Set aside.

Lay half the sliced papaya on the bottom of a large glass or ceramic pan (metal may react with the papaya). Cover the papaya with the steaks. Lay the rest of the papaya slices on top. Cover the dish and refrigerate for 2 to 3 hours.

Preheat the oven to 325 degrees.

Spread the oil in the bottom of a glass baking pan or an enameled casserole. Place a layer of onion slices on top of the oil. Remove the steaks from the refrigerator and season with the salt, pepper, and Worcestershire. Lay the steaks over the onion and cover with the papaya and the tomato. Tightly cover the baking pan or casserole and bake until the meat is tender, 30 to 40 minutes. Remove the dish from the oven and spread the lentils and papaya seeds over the meat. Return the dish to the oven and bake about 15 minutes longer.

Pumpkin Meat Loaf

YIELD: 6 SERVINGS

The pumpkin vine ain't gonna ask your advice about what road to travel.

—Slave proverb

This is a spectacular dish: meat loaf baked and served inside a whole pumpkin!

1 large pumpkin, 3 to 5 pounds
2 pounds lean ground beef
1 tablespoon Worcestershire sauce
1 egg, beaten
¾ cup tomato juice or 1 10½-ounce can condensed tomato soup
¼ cup grated Parmesan cheese
½ cup dry bread crumbs
½ teaspoon garlic powder
½ teaspoon salt
½ teaspoon black pepper

Preheat the oven to 325 degrees.

Carefully cut off the top of the pumpkin so that it can be tightly replaced. Scoop out the seeds and stringy membrane. Combine the ground meat and the remaining ingredients. Stuff the pumpkin with the meat loaf mixture. Set the top back on the pumpkin and bake it for 1 to 1½ hours, or until the outside of the pumpkin feels soft. Remove the pumpkin top and continue cooking for another 10 to 20 minutes, or until the meat loaf is brown.

VEGETABLES AND EGGS

Twice-Baked Sweet Potatoes

YIELD: 8 SERVINGS

When one is very hungry, one doesn't peel the sweet potato. —Caribbean proverb

4 medium sweet potatoes
⅔ cup milk
¼ cup peanut butter
¼ teaspoon ground cinnamon
¼ teaspoon salt
½ teaspoon ground nutmeg
½ cup peanuts

Preheat the oven to 425 degrees.

Arrange the sweet potatoes on a cookie sheet or in a baking pan. Bake until fork-tender, 50 to 60 minutes. Lower the oven heat to 350 degrees. (If using a microwave, arrange the sweet potatoes like the spokes of a wheel with the smaller ends in the middle. Microwave on high for 10 to 15 minutes, or until fork-tender.)

When the sweet potatoes are cool enough to handle, slice each one lengthwise. Leaving the shells intact, scoop out the flesh and put in a bowl. Mash the flesh, then add the milk, peanut butter, cinnamon, and salt and beat until fluffy. Spoon into the shells. Sprinkle with the nutmeg and peanuts and place on a baking sheet.

Bake the sweet potatoes until lightly browned, about 10 minutes. (If using a microwave oven, microwave on medium for 4 minutes.)

Concombre en Daube
(Stewed Cucumbers)

YIELD: 6 SERVINGS

This unusual recipe is the solution for a garden that has produced far more cucumbers than you can pickle or eat in salads.

- **3 tablespoons olive or vegetable oil**
- **1 medium onion, chopped**
- **3 medium tomatoes, peeled and chopped**
- **½ teaspoon salt**
- **½ teaspoon black pepper**
- **¼ teaspoon sugar**
- **3 medium cucumbers, peeled, halved, seeded, and thickly sliced**

In a medium saucepan, heat the oil until it is hot but not smoking and sauté the onion until golden and tender. Add the tomatoes, salt, pepper, and sugar. Stir in the cucumbers. Cover the saucepan and simmer over low heat for 45 minutes.

Metagee

YIELD: 8 SERVINGS

This recipe has as many names and variations as it contains vegetables. Metagee is also called sancoche, sancocho, oildown, and oileen. A top layer of cooked fish or dumplings is sometimes added. I prefer this vegetarian version for the flavor that results when all the different vegetables blend with the coconut milk and cook down to creamy perfection. You can vary the vegetables, as long as the firmer root vegetables stay on the bottom and the more tender vegetables on top.

2 green plantains, peeled
1½ pounds cocoyams or white potatoes, peeled
1½ pounds sweet potatoes, peeled
2 large carrots, peeled
½ pound pumpkin, peeled, seeded, and membrane removed
1 large onion, sliced
6 to 8 okra, ends and stems removed
½ teaspoon dried thyme
1 teaspoon salt
½ teaspoon black pepper
3 cups coconut milk

Cut the peeled vegetables into large pieces. In a heavy covered pot or Dutch oven, layer the vegetables: start with the plantains, then the cocoyams or white potatoes and the sweet potatoes, carrots, pumpkin, onion, and okra. Combine the thyme, salt, and pepper with the coconut milk. Pour half the coconut milk mixture down the sides of the pot containing the vegetables and the rest over the top. Over high heat, bring the vegetables to a boil. Cover, reduce the heat, and simmer until some of the liquid has evaporated and the vegetables on the bottom are fork-tender, about 30 minutes.

Spinach Fritters

YIELD: 4 SERVINGS

Them that eats can say grace. —Slave proverb

1 pound spinach, washed and stems removed
4 tablespoons butter
½ teaspoon dried thyme
⅛ teaspoon dried marjoram
2 tablespoons minced onion
½ teaspoon black pepper
½ teaspoon salt
½ green bell pepper, seeded and diced
1 egg, lightly beaten
Bread crumbs
2 cups vegetable oil

Place the washed, slightly wet spinach in a pot. Add the butter and seasonings. Over low heat, cook the spinach in its own moisture until tender, about 10 minutes. Drain off the excess liquid and chop the spinach finely, then add the bell pepper and the egg. Stir in enough bread crumbs to make a firm consistency and form into 8 to 10 balls.

In a deep skillet, heat the oil until it is hot but not smoking and fry the spinach fritters until brown. Drain on paper towels.

Orange Rice

YIELD: 8 SERVINGS

All the buzzards in the settlement come to the gray mare's funeral. —Slave proverb

2 cups orange juice
1 tablespoon butter
1 tablespoon sugar
1 cup uncooked rice
2 tablespoons orange zest

In a medium saucepan, bring the orange juice to a boil. Stir in the butter, sugar, and rice, combining well, then cover tightly. Simmer the rice over low heat about 18 minutes. Do not lift the cover or stir.

Remove from the heat. Add the orange zest and stir. The rice should be tender and the liquid absorbed.

Pigeon Peas and Rice

YIELD: 8 SERVINGS

This dish is as important to Island cuisine as palm trees and beaches are to Island scenery.

1½ cups dried pigeon peas, picked over
¼ pound salt pork, diced
2 medium onions, chopped
1 stalk celery, chopped
½ cup chopped green bell pepper
1 clove garlic, chopped
6 cups water
½ teaspoon cayenne pepper
½ teaspoon dried thyme
¼ teaspoon black pepper
2 sprigs parsley, chopped
2 cups uncooked rice

Put the peas in a pot, cover with cold water, and bring to a rapid boil. Remove from the heat and set aside for 1 hour. Drain and rinse the peas.

In a Dutch oven or heavy skillet, sauté the salt pork until golden. Remove with a slotted spoon and set aside. Add the onion, celery, bell pepper, and garlic to the skillet. Cook the vegetables over low heat until tender. Return the salt pork to the skillet and add the peas, water, cayenne pepper, thyme, black pepper, and parsley. Bring to a boil, then reduce the heat and simmer until the peas are tender, about 40 minutes. Add the rice and stir. Cover the skillet and simmer over low heat until all the liquid is absorbed, about 30 minutes.

Coo Coo

YIELD: 8 TO 10 SLICES

The history of this recipe is traceable to the Indians of Brazil. No one really knows how coo coo spread to the Islands, although the preparation of this dish is very similar to that of the African mealie meal. Coo coo is usually served as a starchy vegetable side dish, with meat or fish as the main course.

3 cups water
1 teaspoon salt
8 small okra, washed, stemmed, and sliced crosswise
1 cup cornmeal
1 tablespoon butter

In a heavy saucepan, bring the water to a boil. Add the salt and okra. Cover and cook about 10 minutes. Drain the okra, reserving the cooking water. Set the okra aside.

Return 1½ cups of the cooking water to the saucepan and bring it to a boil. Rapidly stir in the cornmeal in a steady stream to form a stiff paste. Stir until the mixture is smooth. Gradually add about ¼ cup more of the cooking water, cover, and cook over low heat about 5 minutes. Butter a mold or loaf pan.

Stir in the cooked okra, adding more water if necessary to make the coo coo smooth. Continue to cook slowly, stirring occasionally, until the mixture is stiff, about 5 minutes. Scrape the coo coo into the mold or loaf pan, let it set for 1 hour, and turn it out onto a plate. Slice before serving.

Ackee and Scrambled Eggs

YIELD: 4 SERVINGS

Ackee is extremely popular in Jamaica and relatively unknown in other parts of the world, except as a specialty item sold in cans. Ackee trees were brought along as cargo to the Caribbean Islands during the days of the slave trade. Legend has it that slaves familiar with the uses of ackee poisoned their masters with the deadly red unripened fruit. Ackee is ripe when it has burst open, showing the yellow, edible fruit inside.

4 large eggs
1 cup canned ackee, drained
½ teaspoon chopped cilantro
2 tablespoons half-and-half or cream
½ teaspoon salt
½ teaspoon black pepper
3 tablespoons butter or margarine

In a medium bowl, beat together until foamy all the ingredients except the butter or margarine. In a skillet, melt the butter. Pour the egg mixture into the skillet, scraping the bottom and sides constantly with a spoon. Remove the skillet from the heat as soon as the eggs have partly set, about 3 minutes. Continue to stir. Serve as soon as the eggs are cooked but still fluffy.

BREADS AND DESSERTS

Bakes

YIELD: ABOUT 2 DOZEN

These crisp fried biscuits traveled from the Islands to America along with slave cooks. Bakes became fried biscuits and were cooked in the grease that was left after fixing a batch of Southern fried chicken.

2 cups all-purpose flour
2 teaspoons baking powder
½ teaspoon salt
2 teaspoons sugar
2 tablespoons shortening
¼ cup cold water
½ cup vegetable oil

In a large mixing bowl, sift together the flour, baking powder, salt, and sugar. With a pastry cutter or fork, cut in the shortening; the mixture should be crumbly. Add the water a little at a time, mixing by hand until a soft dough forms. Knead the dough lightly on a floured board, adding a little more flour if it is too sticky. Pinch off walnut-sized pieces of dough and roll them into balls. Flatten the balls into circles about ½ inch thick. In a heavy skillet, heat the oil until it is hot but not smoking and fry the bakes until golden brown on both sides.

Orange Bread

YIELD: 1 9 × 5-INCH LOAF

This citrus-flavored bread is superb sliced, toasted, and buttered.

2 cups all-purpose flour
4 teaspoons baking powder
½ cup sugar
½ teaspoon salt
1 tablespoon orange zest
1 egg, well beaten
1 cup orange juice
4 tablespoons unsalted butter, melted

Preheat the oven to 350 degrees.

Sift together the flour, baking powder, sugar, salt, and orange zest. Combine the egg with the orange juice and butter and stir slowly into the flour. Pour the batter into a greased 9 × 5-inch loaf pan and bake for 30 minutes, or until a cake tester comes out clean.

Key Lime Pie

YIELD: 1 9-INCH PIE

Key Lime Pie is one of the most popular desserts on the Islands. Authentic Key lime pie has a yellow filling and a pastry crust. The round, beige Key limes are common in the Caribbean and Florida but are more difficult to find in other parts of the United States; however, bottled Key lime juice may be available. Although the taste will be a little different, you can substitute the juice from green limes.

3 jumbo or 4 large eggs, separated
1 14-ounce can sweetened condensed milk
½ cup fresh Key lime or green lime juice, or ½ cup bottled lime juice
½ teaspoon cream of tartar
⅛ teaspoon salt
4 tablespoons sugar
½ teaspoon vanilla extract
1 9-inch unbaked pie crust

Preheat the oven to 350 degrees.

In a medium bowl, with an electric mixer set on medium speed, beat the egg yolks until thick. Add the condensed milk to the beaten yolks and beat until well blended. Add the lime juice and beat again for 2 minutes. Set aside.

In a small bowl, with the electric mixer set on moderate speed, beat the egg whites until frothy. Blend in the cream of tartar and salt. Add the sugar 1 tablespoon at a time. Add the vanilla and beat on high speed until the meringue is glossy and stands in soft peaks when the beaters are withdrawn. Do not overbeat. Add a quarter of the meringue to the filling and combine well. Pour the filling into the pie crust.

Spoon the remaining meringue over the top of the pie, spreading it so that it completely covers the filling and the edges. Bake the pie for 15 minutes, or until the meringue is golden brown. Let the pie cool for 2 hours before refrigerating.

Pineapple Rice Pudding

YIELD: 6 SERVINGS

This is an elegant version of the traditional Spanish rice pudding (arroz con leche). *The fluffy meringue and pineapple-flavored sauce add a Caribbean touch.*

2 cups cooked rice
3 cups milk
⅓ cup plus 2 tablespoons sugar
2 tablespoons butter
½ teaspoon salt
3 eggs, separated
1½ teaspoons vanilla extract
1 20-ounce can crushed pineapple, with juice reserved
½ cup flaked sweetened coconut
1 tablespoon cornstarch
¼ cup packed brown sugar
Pinch salt

Preheat the oven to 325 degrees. Butter a 9 × 13-inch baking dish.

In a medium saucepan, combine the rice, 2½ cups of the milk, ⅓ cup of the sugar, 1 tablespoon of the butter, and the salt. Over moderate heat, stir until thick and creamy, about 20 minutes. Beat the egg yolks with the remaining ½ cup of milk. Add to the rice mixture, cook about 1 minute, and remove from the heat. Stir in 1 teaspoon of the vanilla extract and the pineapple. Refrigerate until cool.

In a small mixing bowl, beat the egg whites until foamy. Gradually add the remaining 2 tablespoons sugar, beating until the whites hold stiff peaks but are not dry. Fold the meringue into the cooled rice mixture and turn into the buttered baking dish. Sprinkle with the coconut. Bake for 20 to 25 minutes.

In a medium saucepan over low heat, mix the pineapple juice with the cornstarch. Stir until the cornstarch is completely dissolved. Add the remaining 1 tablespoon butter, the brown sugar, and the pinch of salt. Cook, stirring frequently, until clear and thickened. Add the remaining ½ teaspoon vanilla extract. Just before serving, drizzle the sauce over the warm pudding.

Matrimony

YIELD: 6 SERVINGS

This is a perfect dessert for a wedding dinner. Starfruit, also called carambola, was once pretty exotic. Now it can be found in most grocery stores. Choose full, firm, yellow fruit with thick, wide ribs to ensure that you're buying the sweetest ones. Starfruit with narrow ribs are as sour as lemons. The starfruit and the oranges in this dessert make a lovely pair.

6 large starfruit
4 oranges, sectioned
1 14-ounce can sweetened condensed milk
½ teaspoon sugar
Ground nutmeg (optional)

Cut off the bottom third of the starfruit. The cross sections of the fruit will be star-shaped. The pulp of the starfruit is very soft and full of seeds. Scoop it out with a spoon and pick out the seeds. Peel and section the orange. Combine the starfruit pulp and the orange sections, then refrigerate. When you are ready to serve, stir in the condensed milk and sugar and sprinkle a little nutmeg on top, if desired.

Baked Banana Custard

YIELD: 8 SERVINGS

This dessert is easy to prepare and light enough to serve after a substantial meal. Enjoy it hot or cold.

4 ripe bananas
5 tablespoons sugar
¼ teaspoon ground nutmeg, plus more for topping the custard
Juice of 1 lime
2 tablespoons butter
½ cup bread crumbs
3 eggs
2 cups milk

Preheat the oven to 325 degrees.

Peel the bananas, removing the threads, and mash until fairly smooth. Add 2 tablespoons of the sugar, the nutmeg, and the lime juice and mix well. Butter a 9 × 13-inch baking dish. Spread the banana mixture evenly in the dish. Cover the bananas with the bread crumbs.

Beat the eggs, gradually beating in the remaining 3 tablespoons of sugar. Heat the milk until warm; do not boil. Slowly add the milk to the beaten eggs, stirring until well blended. Pour the egg mixture over the bananas and sprinkle with nutmeg. Bake until the custard is set, 20 to 25 minutes.

DRINKS

Barley Lemonade

YIELD: 6 TO 8 SERVINGS

½ cup barley
3 quarts plus 1 cup water
2 cups sugar
Zest of 1 lemon
2 lemons, peeled, sectioned, and seeded

In a small saucepan, combine the 3 quarts water and the barley. Over low heat, simmer until the water has been reduced by about a third, 20 to 30 minutes. Pour through a fine sieve into a gallon pitcher or jug. In a small saucepan, combine the sugar, the remaining 1 cup of water, the zest, and the lemon pulp and boil until syrupy. Push the lemon mixture through a sieve, discarding the pulp that remains. Stir the lemon mixture into the barley water. Refrigerate and serve over ice.

Refresco de Coco y Píña
(Coconut and Píneapple Drínk)

YIELD: 3 TO 4 SERVINGS

2 cups coconut milk
2½ cups canned crushed pineapple, drained
2 tablespoons sugar
⅛ teaspoon almond extract

In a blender, combine all the ingredients. Blend at high speed until the mixture is smooth.

Strain through a fine sieve into a pitcher. Refrigerate until thoroughly chilled. Serve over ice.

Refresco de Lechosa
(Milk and Papaya Drink)

YIELD: 3 TO 4 SERVINGS

1 small, ripe papaya (about 12 ounces), peeled, halved, seeded, and coarsely chopped
½ cup coconut milk or whole milk
3 tablespoons lime juice
½ teaspoon lime zest
¼ cup superfine sugar
1 teaspoon vanilla extract
½ cup finely crushed ice
Lime slices for garnish

In a blender, combine all the ingredients except the lime slices. Blend at high speed until smooth and thick. Serve in chilled tumblers, garnished with lime slices.

Peanut and Banana Punch

YIELD: 4 SERVINGS

2 cups whole milk
5 tablespoons sweetened condensed milk
½ banana
3 tablespoons smooth peanut butter
¼ teaspoon ground cinnamon
¼ teaspoon vanilla extract
3 cups crushed ice

Put all the ingredients except the ice in a blender, liquefy, and serve immediately over the crushed ice.

Nectar Punch

YIELD: 4 SERVINGS

1 11½-ounce can banana nectar
1 11½-ounce can apricot nectar
Juice of 1 lime
2 cups club soda

Combine all the ingredients in a large pitcher and refrigerate.

Naranjada
(Orange Cocktail)

YIELD: 4 SERVINGS

Juice of 4 oranges
¼ cup sugar
1½ cups sparkling mineral water or club soda
2 cups crushed ice

Pour the orange juice into a 2-quart pitcher. Add the sugar and stir to mix well. Add the mineral water and crushed ice and stir to combine.

MAKING DO

SLAVE KITCHENS

Would America have been America without her Negro people? —W.E.B. DUBOIS

As a writer, historian, and cook, I often think about the many accomplishments of the African captives who were enslaved in America. Many of their innovative creations have gone unrecognized in history. When I began researching this section of *The African-American Kitchen,* I discovered a large group of women and men whose expertise greatly enhanced American cooking, but whose contributions are seldom noted in cookbooks because they were slaves. These African and African-American cooks concocted dishes that became mainstays in the South and spread across America. They devised ingenious substitutions for ingredients from their homelands that could not be found in America. The real genius of the slave cooks, however, lay in their ability to transform the poor-quality meats and other ingredients they were given for their own consumption into delicious meals.

A slave's daily diet was made up mostly of vegetables, such as wild greens and onions, and cornmeal. "Side" meats, such as salt pork and animal fats were used to enhance the flavor of vegetables rather than as main ingredients. Most of the "soul food" that is part of the African-American culinary heritage is a direct result of slave cooks' "making do" with the few foodstuffs they received.

The plantation kitchen was the slave cooks' domain, and they reigned supreme there. An unhappy cook had many deadly ways of exacting vengeance on the slaveowner, which may be why slave cooks won a little more consideration from the

white household than did other slaves. The landscape architect Frederick Law Olmsted, in a book called *The Cotton Kingdom* about his travels through the South in the mid-1800s, noted that the mistresses of the plantations he visited seemed to know very little about cooking and were happy to leave their kitchens in the hands of their cooks. On some plantations, the cook was also responsible for planning the meals and procuring all the food.

When emancipation came, many slave cooks abandoned their pots and pans to find a new way of life. This left their former masters and mistresses in a quandary, and the popularity of cookbooks greatly increased at this time.

The introduction to the *Picayune Creole Cook Book,* published in New Orleans in 1885, laments "the passing of the faithful old negro cooks—the mammies," which forced

> the ladies of the present day to . . . acquaint themselves thoroughly with the art of cooking . . . to assist them in this, to preserve to future generations the many excellent and matchless recipes of our New Orleans cuisine, to gather these up from the lips of the old Creole negro cooks and the grand old housekeepers who still survive, ere they, too, pass away, and Creole cookery, with all its delightful combinations and possibilities, will have become a lost art.

Here, the craftsmanship the slave cooks brought to Southern kitchens was noted only after slavery came to an end.

Slave cooks created recipes that made the South famous for its food. Although we do not know the names of those who devised the dishes contained in this chapter, their delicious contribution to American cuisine has not been forgotten.

CONDIMENTS

Willie Mae's Green Tomato Chowchow

YIELD: ABOUT 1 GALLON

My Grandmother Willie Mae's chowchow is legendary in my family. It's wonderful with a bowl of black-eyed peas or as a condiment with a mess of greens. Grandma canned her chowchow, but it will keep in an airtight container in the refrigerator for about 7 days.

1 small hot red pepper, washed, trimmed, and seeds removed
4 cups washed, cored, and quartered green tomatoes
4 cups washed, seeded, and quartered green bell peppers
4 cups washed, seeded, and quartered red bell peppers
4 cups chopped white onion
4 cups chopped green cabbage
4 cups apple cider vinegar
1¾ cups sugar
4 tablespoons salt
1 tablespoon celery salt
1 tablespoon mustard seed

Place small quantities of each of the vegetables in a blender or food processor and process until all the vegetables are finely chopped. Set aside.

In a heavy 2-gallon pot, bring to a boil the cider vinegar, sugar, salt, celery seed, and mustard seed.

Add the vegetables to the vinegar mixture. Boil for 10 minutes, stirring occasionally. Put the chowchow in an airtight container and refrigerate immediately.

Watermelon Rind Pickle

YIELD: 3 TO 4 QUARTS

Juicy red watermelons! So sweet and fine! Eat the meat, pickle the rind, save the seeds till planting time! —New Orleans street vendor's cry, circa 1900

For detailed information on canning, refer to Putting Food By *by Janet Greene, Ruth Hertzberg, and Beatrice Vaughn.*

5 pounds watermelon rind (from 2 15-pound watermelons)
1 tablespoon slaked lime (calcium hydroxide), available in drugstores
1 gallon cold water
2 quarts white vinegar
2 cups hot water
5 pounds sugar
1 3-inch stick cinnamon
2 tablespoons whole cloves
2 tablespoons whole allspice
3 or 4 ½-inch pieces gingerroot, peeled (optional)
1 lemon, very thinly sliced (optional)

With a sharp knife, remove the green skin and the red meat of the watermelon, leaving only the thick white rind. Cut the rind into small pieces, about 1 inch square. Put the rind in a large bowl. Mix the slaked lime with the gallon of cold water and pour it over the rind. Soak the mixture in the refrigerator overnight.

Drain the rind and rinse in cold water. Place the pieces in a bowl and cover with ice water. Refrigerate for 1 to 2 hours.

In a large pot, combine the vinegar, hot water, and sugar. Bring the mixture to a boil. Add the cinnamon, cloves, and allspice, and the gingerroot and sliced lemon, if desired. Drain the watermelon rind and add it to the pot.

Simmer, uncovered, for 45 to 60 minutes. The watermelon rind should be transparent and easily pierced with a fork. Spoon the rind into hot sterilized jars and cover with the hot syrup, spices, and lemon rind, distributing the ingredients evenly among the jars. Seal the jars. When cool, label and store in a cool, dark place.

SALADS

Pícníc Potato Salad

YIELD: 6 SERVINGS

There's no law that says you can only eat potato salad in the summertime. But I never think about eating it unless it's hot outside and the smell of hickory smoke from the grill hangs in the air.

5 medium potatoes
4 hard-cooked eggs, diced, plus 1 hard-cooked egg sliced in rounds (optional)
4 stalks celery, diced
3 gherkins, chopped, with 1 tablespoon pickle juice
½ medium white onion, diced
½ teaspoon salt
½ teaspoon black pepper
½ teaspoon sugar
2 whole red pimentos, chopped
5 tablespoons mayonnaise
2 teaspoons prepared mustard
¼ teaspoon paprika

Boil the potatoes until fork-tender, 15 to 20 minutes. Refrigerate until cool, then peel and dice. Add the remaining ingredients except for the paprika and sliced egg. Combine well. Decorate the salad with the sliced egg, if desired, and sprinkle the paprika over the top. Refrigerate.

Fruit Salad

YIELD: 6 SERVINGS

I love the taste and color contrasts a multihued fruit salad adds to a meal.

6 apples, Red or Golden Delicious, Gala, Braeburn
6 bananas, peeled
2 oranges, peeled
2 kiwi fruit, peeled and sliced
1 cup walnuts, coarsely chopped

Dressing:

1 cup heavy cream
1 tablespoon all-purpose flour, mixed with a few drops of water to make a paste
3 tablespoons white vinegar
2 tablespoons butter
2 tablespoons sugar
⅛ teaspoon salt
1 egg white, beaten

Cut all the fruit into small cubes and put into a large bowl. Stir in the nuts.

In a saucepan over low heat, simmer all the dressing ingredients, except the egg white, about 5 minutes, or until the mixture begins to boil. Remove from the heat immediately. Cool until the dressing is barely warm to the touch. Fold in the beaten egg white. Pour the dressing over the fruit, mixing gently to coat each piece. Refrigerate until chilled, about 1 hour.

Cabbage Slaw

YIELD: 8 TO 10 SERVINGS

"Yesterday can take care of itself." —Slave proverb

- **1 medium head cabbage, about 1½ pounds**
- **1 medium onion**
- **½ cup cider vinegar**
- **½ cup sugar**
- **2½ tablespoons vegetable oil**
- **1½ tablespoons prepared mustard**
- **1½ teaspoons salt**
- **½ teaspoon celery seed**

Grate the cabbage and onion and place them in a large bowl. In a small saucepan, bring the remaining ingredients to a boil, stirring often. Pour over the cabbage and onion and toss well. Cover and put in an airtight container. Refrigerate several hours before serving. The slaw will keep well for about a week.

MAIN DISHES

Liver and Onions

YIELD: 6 SERVINGS

The fat cow ain't got much confidence in a butcher. —Slave proverb

¼ cup vegetable oil
1 medium onion, sliced
1 teaspoon salt
1 teaspoon black pepper
1 cup plus 1 tablespoon all-purpose flour
2 pounds calf's liver, sliced
¾ cup water
1 tablespoon steak sauce

In a medium skillet, heat the oil until it is hot but not smoking and sauté the onion until it is tender and golden. Remove the onion from the skillet and set aside. Salt and pepper the liver and dredge in 1 cup of the flour until well coated. Over medium heat, brown the liver on both sides in the oil in the skillet. Add the cooked onion and stir in ½ cup of the water and the steak sauce. Cover and simmer until the liver is fork-tender, 10 to 15 minutes.

In a small bowl, mix the remaining tablespoon of flour with the remaining ¼ cup of water and add it to the skillet to thicken the gravy.

Chítlíns

YIELD: 8 TO 10 SERVINGS

Chitlins, or chitterlings, the small intestines of the pig, are a traditional African-American dish. When it was hog butchering time, the hams, pork chops, and roasts made their way to the master's dinner table. The chitlins went to the slaves. Ingenious African-American cooks prepared them in such a delicious way that the recipe has traveled down through history. My family considers chitlins a special treat on Thanksgiving, Christmas, and New Year's Day. Fix a pot of chitlins, add a side dish of greens and a bottle of hot sauce, and you're ready for a memorable meal.

2 cups white vinegar
2 cups salt
10 pounds chitlins
2 hog maws
2 cups coarsely chopped onion
2 fresh hot cayenne peppers, each about 3 inches long, washed, stemmed, and coarsely chopped
1½ cups coarsely chopped celery
1 teaspoon black pepper
1 green bell pepper, seeded and coarsely chopped
3 cups water

Fill a large basin with cold water and stir in the vinegar and salt. Drop in the chitlins and hog maws and let them soak for 30 minutes. Drain off the water and refill the basin with cold water. Peel off and discard most of the fat from the chitlins and hog maws. Turn the chitlins inside out and peel away the fat there also. Drain off the water and discard the fat. Rinse the meat under cold running water. Soak the chitlins and hog maws in fresh cold water for 1 to 2 hours longer, changing the water several times. Rinse the meats again under cold running water and check the chitlins, inside and out, to make sure they are free of dirt.

Place the chitlins in a large pot with a tight-fitting lid. Add the onion, cayenne peppers, celery, black pepper, green bell pepper, and 3 cups water and bring to a

boil over high heat. Cover the pot, reduce the heat to low, and simmer about 3 hours, or until almost all the liquid has evaporated and the chitlins and hog maws are tender. Remove the cayenne peppers.

VARIATION:

10 pounds cleaned and cooked chitlins (follow recipe above, omitting seasonings), cut into 1½-inch pieces
1 teaspoon salt
1 teaspoon black pepper
1 egg
1 tablespoon water
2 cups cracker meal
1 cup bacon fat for frying

Season the chitlins with the salt and pepper. In a small bowl, beat the egg with the water and dip each chitlin piece in the mixture. Roll the pieces in the cracker meal. In a skillet, heat the bacon fat and fry the chitlins until golden brown. Do not crowd the meat in the pan. Drain on paper towels. Serves 6 to 8.

Tripe

YIELD: 4 SERVINGS

Slaves often were given tripe, a section of a cow's stomach, as well as other poor cuts of meat. Once again, the slaves learned to make do and create a tasty meal.

1 pound honeycomb tripe
1 tablespoon salt
1 onion, chopped
¼ teaspoon black pepper

Wash the tripe and cover it with water in a pot. Add the salt, onion, and pepper. Bring the ingredients to a boil, then lower the heat. Cover and simmer for 1 hour, or until the meat is fork-tender.

Pigs' Feet in Tomato Sauce

YIELD: 4 TO 6 SERVINGS

An old sow knows enough about figures to count her pigs. —Slave proverb

- **6 medium pigs' feet, split**
- **2 tablespoons lemon juice**
- **½ teaspoon salt**
- **½ teaspoon black pepper**
- **3 large onions, chopped**
- **1 clove garlic**
- **2 bay leaves**
- **½ cup white vinegar**
- **3 stalks celery with leaves, chopped**
- **1 cup prepared tomato sauce**

Wash the pigs' feet in cold water and pat dry. Rub each foot with 1 teaspoon of lemon juice and sprinkle with salt and pepper. Place the feet in a medium pot and cover with water. Bring to a boil, reduce the heat, cover, and cook for 30 minutes.

Add the onions, garlic, bay leaves, vinegar, celery, and tomato sauce to the pot. Cover and continue cooking for 1 hour, or until the meat is fork-tender. Add hot water as needed to keep the meat covered throughout the cooking time. Remove the bay leaves before serving.

Fried Squirrel

YIELD: 3 TO 4 SERVINGS

Although there are squirrels in abundance around the pecan trees in my yard, I had no desire to deplete their population in order to try this recipe. I relied instead on an old recipe and my mother's memory of the taste (like the thigh meat of chicken) and preparation of fried squirrel. I included the recipe to preserve it, and because squirrel was once commonly served by slave cooks to their families. My grandmother used this recipe fairly often, especially when the crops had failed or the weather was too cold for a good garden.

1 squirrel, skinned
2 or 3 eggs
1 cup bread crumbs
½ teaspoon salt
½ teaspoon black pepper
½ teaspoon garlic powder
All-purpose flour for thickening batter, plus 2½ tablespoons
Bacon drippings
¾ cup each milk and light cream, mixed

Clean the squirrel and cut into serving pieces. Beat the eggs and add the bread crumbs, salt, pepper, and garlic powder. Stir in enough flour to make a thin batter. Dip the squirrel pieces in the batter until well coated. In a heavy skillet, heat about ½ inch of bacon or beef drippings until very hot. Brown the squirrel pieces on all sides. Pour off any remaining drippings, cover the skillet, and simmer gently until the squirrel is tender, about 1 hour. Add a little water, if necessary, to keep the meat from drying out.

When the squirrel is tender, remove the pieces to a hot platter. Stir 2½ tablespoons of flour into the pan drippings and let the flour brown a little over low heat. Add the mixed milk and cream gradually, stirring constantly until the gravy is thickened. Season to taste. Serve the gravy over the squirrel pieces.

Baked Rabbit

YIELD: 4 SERVINGS

My grandmother and great-grandmother served the wild rabbit the men in the family shot only in the winter months (they believed breeding rabbits shouldn't be eaten). Now you can find commercially raised rabbits year-round in most grocery stores. Rabbit tastes much like the dark meat of chicken. Because rabbits were once plentiful, it was not unusual to find a recipe for rabbit stewed, fried, or baked in the old Southern "receipt" books.

1 3- to 4-pound rabbit, skinned
1½ tablespoons white vinegar
2 teaspoons salt
½ teaspoon black pepper
3 tablespoons butter or margarine
2 medium onions, chopped
1 carrot, diced
2 bay leaves
1 clove garlic, diced
2 stalks celery, diced
1 tablespoon all-purpose flour
3 tablespoons water

Preheat the oven to 350 degrees.

Wash the rabbit and cut into serving pieces. Place the rabbit in a bowl and cover it with water. Add the vinegar and 1 teaspoon of the salt. Refrigerate for 1 hour.

Drain off the liquid. In a medium skillet, heat the butter or margarine. Season the rabbit pieces with the remaining salt and pepper. Brown the rabbit pieces on both sides. Put the rabbit in a casserole or roasting pan. Add the onions, carrot, bay leaves, garlic, and celery. With the tablespoon of flour and the 3 tablespoons of water, make a paste. Stir it into the liquid surrounding the rabbit to thicken it. Cover the casserole or roasting pan tightly and bake for 1 to 1½ hours, until the meat is fork-tender.

Baked Chicken with Cornbread Dressing

YIELD: 8 SERVINGS

Setting hens don't have a taste for fresh eggs. —Slave proverb

1 teaspoon salt
1 teaspoon black pepper
1 teaspoon dried sage
1 teaspoon garlic powder
1 teaspoon dried thyme
1 5- to 7-pound roasting chicken
2 bay leaves
3 stalks celery, chopped
2 large onions, chopped

Dressing:

4 cups crumbled cornbread
1 cup day-old bread or dinner rolls
½ cup sliced mushrooms
½ teaspoon dried sage
½ teaspoon dried thyme
4 tablespoons butter or margarine, melted
1 teaspoon salt
¼ teaspoon black pepper
2½ cups chicken broth

Parsley sprigs

Combine the salt, pepper, sage, garlic powder, and thyme and rub the seasonings inside the chicken and on the skin. Put the chicken in a large, heavy pot. Add the bay leaves, celery, and onions and enough water to cover. Bring the ingredients to

a boil, then reduce the heat, cover, and simmer until the chicken is tender, about 1 hour.

Remove the chicken from the broth and set on a greased baking sheet. Strain the broth through a sieve, reserving 2½ cups of the broth and separately reserving the vegetables to use in the dressing. Discard the bay leaves.

Preheat the oven to 400 degrees and place the chicken in a shallow roasting pan.

To prepare the dressing, combine all the dressing ingredients, except the broth, in a baking pan. Add the celery and onions that were simmered with the chicken, then add the broth until the dressing is moist but not soupy, with a consistency of mush.

Bake the chicken and the dressing, uncovered, for 30 to 40 minutes, or until the chicken is golden brown and the dressing is firm but still moist.

Serve the chicken in the center of a platter surrounded by the dressing and garnished with parsley.

Chicken Pie

YIELD: 8 SERVINGS

You can't tell much about chicken pie until you get through the crust. —Slave proverb

1 4- to 5-pound chicken, cut into serving pieces
½ cup minced onion
½ cup minced celery
2 bay leaves
1 teaspoon dried thyme
1 teaspoon dried sage
1 teaspoon salt
1 teaspoon black pepper
3 tablespoons butter
3 tablespoons all-purpose flour
1 cup milk

Crust:

2 cups all-purpose flour
2 teaspoons baking powder
1 teaspoon salt
4 tablespoons butter
1 egg
2 cups milk

To prepare the chicken: Place the chicken in a pot with the onion, celery, bay leaves, thyme, sage, salt, and pepper. Cover with water and boil until cooked through, about 45 minutes. Strain the broth, reserving 2 cups along with the vegetables. Discard the bay leaves. When cool enough to handle, remove the chicken from the bones and put the meat in a 12 × 15-inch baking dish or a deep casserole.

In a small saucepan, melt the 3 tablespoons butter, stir in the flour, and blend. Add the reserved broth and the milk to the flour mixture and cook until it becomes

a thin gravy, about 5 minutes. Add the reserved vegetables and pour the gravy over the chicken.

To prepare the crust: Preheat the oven to 350 degrees. Sift together the dry ingredients, then cut in the butter. In a small bowl, beat together the egg and milk and stir the mixture into the flour mixture until smooth. You will have a thin batter. Pour over the chicken and gravy and bake for 1½ hours.

Chicken and Dumplings

YIELD: 4 TO 6 SERVINGS

Lazy folks' stomachs don't get tired. —Slave proverb

1 3- to 4-pound chicken, cut into serving pieces
½ teaspoon salt
½ teaspoon black pepper
⅛ teaspoon ground nutmeg
¼ teaspoon sweet paprika
All-purpose flour for dredging
6 tablespoons bacon drippings, butter, or margarine
1 medium onion, chopped
1 green bell pepper, seeded and diced
1 stalk celery, chopped
2 carrots, sliced
1 bay leaf
6 cups water
1 cup fresh, frozen, or canned whole-kernel corn

Dumplings:

1¼ cups all-purpose flour
1½ teaspoons baking powder
1 teaspoon salt
1 egg, beaten
½ cup milk
1 tablespoon margarine or butter, melted

Season the chicken with the salt, pepper, nutmeg, and paprika, then dredge in flour. In a skillet, heat 2 tablespoons of the bacon drippings, butter, or margarine and cook the onion over moderate heat until golden. Remove the onion from the skillet and reserve. Add the remaining 4 tablespoons of shortening to the skillet. Return

the heat to moderate and brown the chicken in batches on both sides. As they brown, place the chicken pieces in a large pot. Add the onion, green bell pepper, celery, carrots, bay leaf, and water. Bring to a boil. Reduce the heat, cover, and simmer for 30 minutes.

While the chicken is simmering, prepare the dumplings. Sift together in a bowl the flour, baking powder, and salt. Add the egg, milk, and melted shortening. Blend the ingredients until they make a soft dough.

Remove the lid from the pot and add the corn to the chicken. Drop the dumpling batter by tablespoonfuls into the pot. Cover the pot and simmer 20 minutes. Do not remove the cover or stir. Remove the bay leaf before serving.

Southern Fried Chicken

YIELD: 4 TO 6 SERVINGS

Southern fried chicken has been a favorite dish for more than 150 years. There are as many variations on this recipe as there are people who like the dish, but the chicken should always be brown and crisp outside and moist and tender inside.

1 2- to 3-pound chicken, cut into serving pieces
Milk to cover chicken, 3 to 4 cups
½ teaspoon Tabasco sauce
1½ cups all-purpose flour
1 teaspoon salt
1 teaspoon black pepper
1 teaspoon hot or sweet paprika
1 teaspoon garlic powder
1 teaspoon poultry seasoning
2 cups vegetable oil
2 tablespoons butter or margarine

Put the chicken pieces in a large mixing bowl and add milk to cover. Add the Tabasco and refrigerate for 1 hour.

Combine the flour, salt, pepper, paprika, garlic powder, and poultry seasoning in a heavy paper bag or large plastic bag. Shake to blend. Remove the chicken pieces from the milk, shaking off the excess liquid. Drop the chicken pieces one at a time into the seasoned flour and shake until well coated. Using a large heavy skillet (preferably cast iron), heat the oil and butter or margarine until a pinch of flour sizzles when sprinkled on top. Reduce the heat to moderate and cook the chicken pieces in batches (don't crowd them!). Continue cooking until the pieces are golden brown on each side, 25 to 30 minutes. Drain on paper towels.

Chicken with Peaches

YIELD: 6 SERVINGS

The peaches and orange juice give this chicken a fresh new taste, a little sweet and slightly tangy. The finished dish looks pretty, too.

1 3- to 4-pound chicken, cut up
1 cup all-purpose flour
1 teaspoon dried sage
1 teaspoon dried thyme
2 teaspoons salt
1 teaspoon black pepper
1½ cups vegetable oil
2½ cups sliced canned peaches
1½ cups orange juice
3 tablespoons packed brown sugar
3 tablespoons white vinegar
1½ teaspoons ground nutmeg
1½ teaspoons dried basil
2 cloves garlic, chopped

Wash the chicken pieces and pat dry. On a plate, combine the flour, sage, thyme, salt, and pepper. Dredge the chicken pieces in the seasoned flour. In a heavy skillet, heat the oil until it is hot but not smoking and brown the chicken well. Remove the chicken to a platter. Pour off the grease but reserve the pan drippings.

In a saucepan, combine the remaining ingredients. Cover tightly and simmer for 10 minutes. Add one third of the fruit sauce to the pan drippings in the skillet and simmer over low heat, stirring. Return the chicken to the pan and cover with the remaining fruit sauce. Cover tightly. Simmer for 20 minutes, or until the chicken is done.

Southern Baked Ham

YIELD: 12 TO 15 SERVINGS

I remember reading about this recipe in a novel set in the South. I thought it was strange to pour Coke over a ham. Although the story was fiction, the recipe was authentic and definitely a Southern creation. Some hams are so salty that I simmer them in a large pot of water about 20 minutes before baking them this way.

1 14- to 16-pound cured ham
2 12-ounce cans Coca-Cola
Pineapple rings, red cherries, and cloves for garnish

Preheat the oven to 300 degrees.

Starting 4 inches from the end of the ham, trim off the skin and fat, leaving about ¼ inch of fat. Place the ham in a large heavy pan with a lid. Pour 1 can of Coca-Cola over the ham. Add ½ inch of water. Cover tightly and bake for 1 hour. Remove the cover. Pour the other can of Coca-Cola over the ham. Leave uncovered and bake for another 2 hours.

Score the cooked ham in a large crisscross pattern. Place a pineapple ring with a cherry pierced by a clove in each scored segment. Let the ham sit in a warm place for 30 minutes before serving so that it will carve easily.

Ham Steak and Red-Eye Gravy

YIELD: 4 BREAKFAST SERVINGS

The penitentiary has some folks in it that knew how to call hogs too well.

—Slave proverb

1 center slice country ham, about 3/8 inch thick
1 tablespoon vegetable oil
1 cup water
1 to 2 tablespoons brewed black coffee (optional)

Soak the ham in cold water for 30 minutes to an hour to remove the salt. Drain and pat dry. In a heavy skillet, heat the vegetable oil until it is hot but not smoking. Cook the ham over moderate to low heat about 20 minutes, turning occasionally, or until tender. Remove the ham from the skillet and set aside in a warm place.

Add the water to the skillet and cook, stirring to loosen all the browned particles and pieces of meat. Boil 5 minutes. Add 1 or 2 tablespoons of coffee to darken the gravy. This goes well with eggs or over grits or biscuits.

Fried Fish

YIELD: 1 SERVING PER 2 OR 3 SMALL FISH

Ground worms aren't anxious for the fish to bite. —Slave proverb

2 or 3 small fish (mackerel, whitings, porgies, or butterfish) per person
1 cup all-purpose flour
1 cup cornmeal
1 teaspoon salt
1 teaspoon black pepper
1 teaspoon poultry seasoning
1½ cups shortening

Wash and clean the fish, making sure the fins and all scales are removed. In a flat dish, combine the flour, cornmeal, salt, pepper, and poultry seasoning and dredge the fish in the flour mixture until well coated.

In a skillet, heat the shortening until it is very hot but not smoking. Fry the fish until browned on both sides, about 3 minutes per side. Drain on paper towels.

Okra Gumbo

YIELD: 4 SERVINGS

The preparation of okra is a gift to America from African cooks who were enslaved here. Both the word gumbo, *which means "okra" in some African dialects, and the recipe of the same name are African imports. Gumbo was first introduced to New Orleans cuisine by slave cooks. Now Louisiana is famous for its gumbos. There are as many variations of this recipe as there are cooks, from difficult roux-based gumbos to simpler okra-based ones. All are delicious served with a bowl of hot, fluffy rice.*

¾ cup (1½ sticks) butter or margarine
3 cups chopped onion
1 clove garlic, minced
8 cups sliced okra
7 cups chopped tomatoes
2 tablespoons dried parsley
1 teaspoon sweet paprika
½ teaspoon black pepper
1 teaspoon salt
Juice of ½ lemon
1 tablespoon sugar
1 teaspoon Worcestershire sauce
3 tablespoons ketchup

In a large skillet, melt 4 tablespoons of the butter or margarine. Sauté the onion and garlic until golden, about 5 minutes. Remove the onion and garlic with a slotted spoon and set aside. Melt the remaining butter or margarine in the skillet, add the okra, and simmer for 10 minutes, stirring often. Add the remaining ingredients, cover, and simmer, stirring occasionally, 30 to 40 minutes.

Southern Succotash

YIELD: 4 SERVINGS

Corn mixed with beans became a staple in the South as the Civil War dragged on through the 1860s and in its aftermath, as times became harder and harder. Newly freed blacks may have fared a little better than newly poor whites because they already knew how to make do with the food that was available. Succotash, originally a Native American recipe, became a popular main dish. Succotash is delicious, especially with buttered cornbread.

1 cup dried baby lima beans
3 cups water
1 teaspoon salt
1 28-ounce can whole tomatoes with liquid
¼ teaspoon dried thyme
2 small bay leaves
2 tablespoons chopped green bell pepper
1 tablespoon bacon fat
1 cup fresh, frozen, or canned corn kernels
1 tablespoon sugar

Put all the ingredients except the corn and sugar in a large pot. Bring the ingredients to a boil. Cover and simmer 1½ hours, adding more water as needed to cover the beans and vegetables.

Stir in the corn and sugar. Cover and cook another 25 minutes, stirring occasionally.

Baked Macaroní and Cheese

YIELD: 8 SERVINGS

James Hemings, President Thomas Jefferson's black slave chef, was among the first cooks in America to serve macaroni. His recipe was fairly simple:

> Break macaroni in small pieces, there should be 2 cupfuls, and boil in salted water until tender. Grate ¼ pound of cheese and mix with the same amount of butter. Stir into the macaroni and bake in a moderate oven until the cheese is thoroughly melted.

This version of macaroni and cheese is also an old one.

6 cups water
1 tablespoon salt
2 cups elbow macaroni
¼ cup plus 2 tablespoons butter, softened
2 large eggs
2 cups evaporated milk
1 teaspoon salt
2 dashes Tabasco sauce
1 pound extra-sharp cheddar cheese, grated and mixed with ½ cup grated American cheese
½ teaspoon sweet paprika

Preheat the oven to 350 degrees.

Put the water and salt in a heavy saucepan and bring to a boil. Slowly stir in the macaroni. Boil for 12 minutes, stirring constantly. The macaroni should be firm but tender. Pour the macaroni into a colander and rinse with a little cold water. Drain. Toss the macaroni with the butter and set aside.

In a small bowl, beat the eggs until light yellow. Add the milk, salt, and Tabasco sauce. In a large buttered casserole dish, alternate layers of the cooked macaroni with layers of the mixed cheeses, ending with the cheeses on top. Pour the egg mixture slowly and evenly over the macaroni and cheese. Sprinkle with the paprika. Bake for 30 to 40 minutes, until the custard is set and the top is bubbly and golden brown.

VEGETABLES

Cabbage with Cracklings

YIELD: 6 SERVINGS

Often all the slaves had for meat rations was pork skin. The slaves cooked the skin in a skillet until it crackled; hence the name for the delicious bits of skin and crisp meat that remained after the fat had been rendered from the pork skin. Slave cooks mixed the cracklings into their cornbread batter or cooked them with vegetables. Many grocery stores sell pork cracklings, and you can make your own at home. In a heavy skillet over moderate heat, cook 1 cup of chopped salt pork or slab bacon for 10 minutes, until it is crisp and brown. Drain and reserve the fat for frying. The crisp bits that are left are the cracklings.

1 head green cabbage, about 3 pounds, washed
1 medium onion, sliced
2 teaspoons bacon fat
½ cup cracklings
1 teaspoon salt
¼ teaspoon black pepper
1 teaspoon dried thyme
½ teaspoon sugar
1 cup water
1 teaspoon white vinegar

Core and coarsely chop the cabbage, discarding any yellow leaves. In a large pot, brown the onion in the bacon fat until golden. Add the cabbage, cracklings, salt, pepper, thyme, sugar, and water. Cover and cook over low heat 20 minutes, stirring often. Mix in the vinegar and cook the cabbage for another 3 minutes.

Fried Green Tomatoes

YIELD: 4 SERVINGS

Some food historians believe that recipes using tomatoes were introduced to America by slave cooks. Fried green tomatoes are traditionally served with bacon and eggs at breakfast-time in the South.

4 green tomatoes, stemmed and sliced ½ inch thick
½ teaspoon salt
½ teaspoon black pepper
½ teaspoon garlic powder
4 tablespoons (½ stick) butter
All-purpose flour for dredging
2 eggs, beaten

Season the tomatoes with the salt, pepper, and garlic powder. In a skillet, melt the butter. Dredge the tomato slices in flour, dip them into the eggs, and dredge them again in the flour. Sauté the battered slices in the butter, cooking 3 to 5 minutes on one side; then turn and cook until golden brown on both sides.

New Potatoes and Snap Beans

YIELD: 6 SERVINGS

The dinner bell is always in tune. —Slave proverb

- **2 pounds fresh beans (snap beans, green beans, or string beans)**
- **1 small ham hock**
- **½ medium onion, sliced**
- **1 pound small new potatoes**
- **½ teaspoon salt**
- **½ teaspoon black pepper**
- **½ teaspoon dried thyme**

Snap the ends off the beans, string them, and break them into pieces 2 or 3 inches long. Put the ham hock in a large pot with water to cover. Turn the heat to moderate and cook the ham hock, covered, about 20 minutes. Add the beans and onion, cover, and continue cooking.

Wash the potatoes thoroughly. Peel away a band of skin around the middle of each potato. Place the potatoes on top of the beans, sprinkling them well with the salt, pepper, and thyme. Cover the pot and continue cooking until the potatoes and beans are tender when tested with a fork, 10 to 15 minutes. Add more water if needed. Taste a few beans and add salt and pepper if desired.

Old-Fashioned String Beans

YIELD: 4 SERVINGS

Don't say more with your mouth than your back can stand. —Slave proverb

4 slices lean bacon, diced
½ cup thinly sliced scallions
1 pound green beans, washed, snapped, and strings removed
1 tablespoon cold water
1 teaspoon salt
¼ teaspoon black pepper
1½ teaspoons red-wine vinegar
2 tablespoons finely cut fresh mint leaves

In a large skillet, fry the bacon, turning the pieces frequently until brown and crisp. Drain on a paper towel. Cook the scallions in the bacon fat over moderate heat for 3 to 4 minutes, until they are soft but not brown. Add the beans to the skillet, stirring them until they are well coated with the bacon fat. Add the tablespoon of water and cover the pan tightly. Cook over low heat for 5 minutes, then uncover the pan and continue to cook until the beans are crisp-tender. Sprinkle the beans with the salt and pepper, stir in the vinegar, and remove from the heat. Put the beans in a serving dish, crumble the bacon, and sprinkle the beans with the bacon pieces and mint.

Beans and Neck Bones

YIELD: 4 SERVINGS

Fat hogs don't have much to brag on when killing time comes. —Slave proverb

2 pounds fresh pork neck bones, cracked and washed
1 cup dried pinto beans or lima beans, soaked overnight in water to cover
1 teaspoon salt
2 medium onions, chopped
½ teaspoon dried thyme
6 cups water

Drain the soaking water from the beans and discard any that are discolored. Combine the beans and the remaining ingredients in a large pot. Cover and bring to a boil. Lower the heat and simmer 1½ to 2 hours, stirring frequently and adding more water as needed. The water should just cover the meat and beans throughout the cooking time. Taste and correct the seasonings.

Hoppín' John

YIELD: 10 SERVINGS

Black-eyed peas were transported from Africa to the West Indies and then into the Carolinas before the 1700s. Black-eyed peas are said to bring good luck in the New Year. Hoppin' John is an African dish that has been adapted for American tastes and is commonly served on New Year's Day.

Some say the dish got its name from a corruption of the word bahatta-kachang, *which is of African origin. Others say the name comes from the tradition of having the children of the family hop around the table once for luck before eating the dish. All I know is that you're a lucky person if you can sit down to a dish of Hoppin' John.*

1 pound dried black-eyed peas, picked over and soaked overnight in 6 cups water
½ pound smoked ham hocks
1 onion, sliced
1 whole hot cayenne pepper
1 teaspoon salt
1 cup cooked rice

Place the peas and water in a pot over moderate heat and add the ham hocks, onion, hot pepper, and salt. Bring to a boil, reduce the heat to low, cover, and simmer for 1 to 1½ hours, or until the peas and meat are tender. Remove the hot pepper.

Remove skin and bones from the hocks and cut the meat into small pieces. Return the meat to the pot. Add the cooked rice to the pot and heat about 5 minutes.

Creamed Corn

YIELD: 6 SERVINGS

For years, my only acquaintance with creamed corn was with the canned variety. I didn't taste fresh creamed corn until I became an adult. An older friend showed me how to prepare the dish. The milk contained in the kernels of fresh corn gives this dish a wonderful taste. Try it; you'll never want canned "cream-style" corn again.

5 ears fresh corn (white is best)
½ to 1 cup milk, as needed
½ cup (1 stick) butter
1 teaspoon salt
⅛ teaspoon white pepper
1 teaspoon cornstarch, as needed
1 teaspoon cold milk, as needed

Shuck the corn and remove the silks carefully. You may want to use a soft brush so as not to break open the grains. Rinse thoroughly. Pointing the end of the cob down into a bowl, use a sharp knife to gently remove the kernels. Do not try to remove the corn down to the cob all at once. Slice off one third of the grain all around the cob, then another third. Cut the last third off close to the cob, then scrape the remaining corn milk into the bowl.

Put the corn and corn milk into a heavy skillet. Rinse out the bowl with a little water to get all the corn milk. If the corn is dry, add ½ cup milk to the skillet. If the corn is still dry, add a little more milk, up to another ½ cup.

Add the butter, salt, and pepper to the skillet. Cover and simmer slowly for 10 minutes, stirring often.

The corn will become tender, and the sauce should thicken to the consistency of cream. If it is still watery, mix 1 teaspoon each of cornstarch and cold milk in a bowl. Add the cornstarch mixture to the corn while stirring. Simmer for another 5 minutes, stirring often.

Fríed Corn

YIELD: 4 SERVINGS

Fried corn has become my oldest sister's specialty. Some recipes call for bacon fat instead of butter, but I think her version gives the corn a better flavor.

½ cup (1 stick) plus 4 tablespoons butter
4 cups fresh corn kernels
1 cup sugar
½ teaspoon salt

In a medium skillet, melt the ½ cup butter. Add the corn, sugar, and salt and stir well. Dot with the remaining 4 tablespoons of butter. Cook over low heat for 15 minutes, stirring frequently.

Corn Pudding

YIELD: 4 SERVINGS

Heap of good cotton stalks get chopped up from associating with weeds.
—Slave proverb

2 eggs
4 tablespoons butter, melted
1 cup milk
3 tablespoons sugar
2 cups cooked corn kernels
2 tablespoons all-purpose flour
½ teaspoon ground nutmeg
1 teaspoon salt
½ teaspoon black pepper

Preheat the oven to 350 degrees.

In a large mixing bowl, beat the eggs. Stir in the melted butter. Add the milk and sugar, combining well. Add the remaining ingredients and blend well. Pour the pudding into a greased 1-quart baking dish. Bake for 45 minutes, or until the custard is set and a knife inserted in the center comes out clean.

Honey-Baked Onions

YIELD: 8 SERVINGS

Ain't much difference between a yellowjacket and a hornet when they both get under your clothes.

—Slave proverb

4 large sweet white onions
1½ cups tomato juice
1½ cups water
2 tablespoons melted butter
6 teaspoons honey

Preheat the oven to 325 degrees.

Peel the onions and discard the skin, then cut in half. Arrange the onions cut side up in a buttered baking dish. In a bowl, combine the remaining ingredients. Pour the sauce over the onions, brushing them to coat. Bake for 1 hour, or until the onions are soft.

Mustard and Turnip Greens

YIELD: 8 TO 10 SERVINGS

Greens flavored with a "side meat" such as ham hocks or fatback were often served by slave cooks to their families as a main dish. When no side meat was available, bacon fat or a ham bone was used. Sometimes greens and vegetables with different flavors were mixed. Pot liquor, the highly seasoned liquid that is left after the greens cook down, is full of vitamins and minerals. If greens were served one day, the leftover pot liquor and a pan of cornbread often made the meal for the next. And the old song, "Ham bone, ham bone, where you been? Around the world and back again," refers to the slaves' practice of sharing a ham bone to flavor a pot of greens or beans, around the slave quarters and back to the owner of the ham bone.

2 ham hocks
2 quarts water
3 pounds mustard greens
4 pounds turnip greens
2 teaspoons sugar
1 teaspoon Tabasco sauce

Place the ham hocks in a large pot. Cover with the water. Bring to a boil, then reduce the heat and simmer, covered, for 2 hours.

Cut the tough stems and yellow leaves from the greens and discard. Gently rub the leaves with your fingers under warm running water until clean. Cut the greens into large pieces. Let the leaves soak in warm, salted water for 10 minutes. Rinse with cool water and drain in a colander.

Skim any fat from the liquid in which the ham hocks were cooked. Remove the hocks and cut the meat into bite-size pieces, discarding the skin and bones. Return the meat to the pot and add the sugar and Tabasco sauce. Add as many greens as will fit in the pot. Cover and cook down until the greens are wilted, then add more greens until all the greens are in the pot. Continue cooking, covered, about 1½ hours.

Greens and Turnips

YIELD: 4 TO 6 SERVINGS

Turnip tops don't tell you the size of the turnip. —Slave proverb

3 pounds fresh turnip greens
1 pound white turnips, peeled and diced
1 quart water
¼ pound salt pork, sliced
1 teaspoon salt
¼ teaspoon black pepper

Cut the tough stems and yellow leaves from the greens and discard. Gently clean the greens under warm running water and cut them into large pieces. Let the leaves soak in warm, salted water for 10 minutes. Rinse with cool water and drain in a colander.

Put the turnips and greens in a large pot and add water to cover. Cover and simmer over low heat. In a small skillet, fry the salt pork until brown, about 5 minutes. Pour the meat and its fat onto the vegetables. Add the salt and pepper and cover. Simmer over low heat for 2 hours, or until the greens are tender.

Greens and Okra

YIELD: 6 TO 8 SERVINGS

Waiting on the table is a powerful way to work up an appetite. —Slave proverb

2 cups chopped ham
3 cups water
4 bunches collard greens
½ tablespoon salt
½ teaspoon sugar
1 or 2 dried cayenne pepper pods to taste
8 to 12 small okra, stemmed

In a heavy pot or Dutch oven, simmer the ham in the water until it is tender and the fat dissolves, 15 to 20 minutes.

Cut the tough stems and yellow leaves from the greens and discard. Gently rub the leaves with your fingers under warm running water. Cut the greens into large pieces. Let the leaves soak in warm, salted water for 10 minutes. Rinse with cool water and drain in a colander.

Add the salt, sugar, and peppers to the ham, then add the greens. Stir every 15 minutes until the greens are wilted but not quite tender, 30 to 45 minutes. Layer the okra on top of the greens. Cover and continue cooking the greens and okra for 20 minutes or until tender, stirring occasionally and adding hot water as needed to prevent the greens from sticking.

Glazed Yellow Turnips

YIELD: 6 SERVINGS

Yellow turnips have a sweeter flavor if selected after the first fall frost.

2½ cups peeled diced turnips
3 tablespoons margarine or butter
3 tablespoons light corn syrup
¼ teaspoon ground nutmeg
Salt and black pepper to taste

Put the turnips in a saucepan and cover with water. Boil until tender, 15 to 20 minutes. Drain. In a skillet over medium heat, melt the margarine or butter. Add the turnips, corn syrup, nutmeg, salt, and pepper. Cook, stirring frequently, about 10 minutes, or until the turnips are lightly browned.

Candied Yams

YIELD: 4 SERVINGS

Eating yams makes you smile all over. —Slave proverb

2 large yams or sweet potatoes, peeled and sliced ½ inch thick
1 teaspoon ground cinnamon
½ cup sugar
½ teaspoon ground nutmeg
2 tablespoons margarine or butter
⅔ cup evaporated milk
⅓ cup water

Preheat the oven to 350 degrees.

Layer half the yams or sweet potatoes in a greased baking dish. Combine the cinnamon, sugar, and nutmeg. Sprinkle half the mixture over the yams. Dot the yams with half the butter. Layer on the rest of the yams, sprinkle with the remaining sugar mixture, and dot with the remaining butter. Mix the milk and water and pour over the yams. Cover and bake for 45 minutes.

Increase the oven temperature to 400 degrees. Uncover the casserole and bake for another 10 minutes, until the yams are golden brown and tender.

RICE

Gullah Rice

YIELD: 4 SERVINGS

Many West Africans were enslaved on the Sea Islands off the coasts of Georgia and South Carolina, most planting and harvesting rice. Linguists have documented more than 30 different tribes and languages on the Sea Islands. To communicate with each other and with the white overseers, the captives devised a combination of African dialects and English which was called Gullah. Because Gullah was not a written language, much of it has been lost. However, remnants of the language and of the Sea Island culture, which is strongly rooted in African traditions, still survive among the descendants of the African captives.

1 cup uncooked rice
2½ cups water
½ teaspoon salt
¼ cup shelled roasted red pistachios
¼ cup minced celery
2 tablespoons margarine or butter

Rinse the rice in a colander under cold running water. Drain. Put the water and salt in a medium saucepan. Add the rice, pistachios, celery, and margarine or butter and bring to a boil. Cover the saucepan and reduce the heat to low. Simmer for 15 minutes, stirring occasionally, until the rice is tender and the water is absorbed.

Jefferson Rice

(Pilau with Pine Nuts and Pistachios)

YIELD: 4 TO 6 SERVINGS

Thomas Jefferson, America's third president, lived a life of great comfort at Monticello, his plantation in Virginia. His well-being was ensured by numerous slaves, including the chef James Hemings and his daughter Sally. Whether Jefferson fathered Sally Hemings's son, Thomas Woodson, and her five other children, two of whom died in infancy, has long been a matter of hot debate among historians. James and Sally Hemings traveled to France with Jefferson in 1785 when he was appointed minister to France. When Jefferson returned in 1789, James had received extensive training in French cuisine and Sally was pregnant with Thomas.

Together Hemings and Jefferson created dishes that introduced an exciting new cuisine to America. "Thomas Jefferson came home from France so Frenchified that he abjured his native victuals," said his political rival Patrick Henry. In fact, Hemings creatively combined the elements of French cuisine with American cooking. For Jefferson and his guests he prepared macaroni, cornbread stuffing, waffles, and ice cream, unusual dishes at that time. Hemings also introduced the use of almonds, raisins, and vanilla. You could say that Hemings cooked his way to freedom. In 1793, Jefferson signed a document that emancipated Hemings if he promised to train a new chef for Monticello.

1 cup uncooked rice
1 cup fresh or canned chicken stock
1 cup water
4 tablespoons butter
1 teaspoon salt
½ cup pine nuts
¼ cup shelled unsalted pistachios
¼ teaspoon ground mace

In a colander, rinse the rice under cold running water. Drain. In a heavy saucepan over high heat, bring the chicken stock, water, 1 tablespoon of the butter, and ½

teaspoon of the salt to a boil. Stir in the rice, cover tightly, and simmer over very low heat about 20 minutes, or until the rice is tender and the grains have absorbed all the liquid.

In a heavy skillet over moderate heat, melt the remaining 3 tablespoons of butter. Stir in the pistachios and sauté until they are a delicate golden color. Remove the skillet from the heat.

Put the cooked rice in a serving bowl and fluff it with a fork. Scrape the nuts over the rice and toss gently. Sprinkle the pilau with the mace and the remaining ½ teaspoon of salt.

Red Rice

YIELD: 6 SERVINGS

Promising talk don't cook rice. —Gullah proverb

- **6 slices lean bacon**
- **1 cup finely chopped onion**
- **½ red bell pepper, seeded and finely chopped**
- **1 cup uncooked rice**
- **⅛ teaspoon Tabasco sauce**
- **1 teaspoon sweet paprika**
- **1 teaspoon sugar**
- **1 teaspoon salt**
- **1 cup chopped drained canned tomatoes**
- **1½ cups cold water**

In a heavy skillet, fry the bacon until crisp and brown. Drain on paper towels, then crumble and set aside.

Pour off all but about 4 tablespoons of the fat remaining in the skillet and add the onion and red bell pepper. Cook over medium heat, stirring frequently, for about 5 minutes. The onion should be soft but not brown. Add the rice and stir to coat the grains with the fat. Stir in the Tabasco sauce, paprika, sugar, salt, tomatoes, and water. Bring the mixture to a boil over high heat, cover tightly, and reduce the heat to very low. Simmer about 20 minutes, or until all the liquid has evaporated and the rice is tender. Remove the skillet from the heat and set aside, covered, for 10 minutes. Serve the rice in a bowl with the crumbled bacon on top.

EGGS

Breakfast Casserole

YIELD: 6 SERVINGS

Rich and poor, black and white,
Lutheran and Campbellite,
Jews and Southern Jesuits,
All acknowledge buttered grits.

—Roy Blount, Jr., "One Fell Soup"

1 cup white hominy grits, or white hominy quick grits
2 slices bacon, fried until crisp and crumbled
4 tablespoons butter or margarine
½ teaspoon salt
½ teaspoon black pepper
6 eggs

Heat the oven to 350 degrees.

Prepare the grits according to the package directions. Stir in the bacon and 2 tablespoons of the butter or margarine. Pour the grits mixture into an ungreased 7 × 11-inch baking dish. With the back of a spoon, make 6 depressions in the grits, about 2 inches apart. Carefully break 1 egg into each depression. Melt the remaining 2 tablespoons of butter and pour over the eggs. Sprinkle with the salt and pepper. Bake, uncovered, for 15 minutes, or until the eggs are done.

Eggs and Green Onions

YIELD: 6 SERVINGS

A friend told me he always felt special when his mother fixed eggs and green onions for breakfast—that is, until his cousins came for a visit. They informed him that eggs and green onions was poor folks' food. My friend said he never realized how poor he was until they told him. I think this is a special breakfast, fit for a king; and now so does he.

2 tablespoons butter
12 scallions (green onions), including tops, chopped fine
6 eggs
¼ cup light cream
½ teaspoon salt
⅛ teaspoon black pepper
1 cup cold cooked rice

In a skillet over low heat, melt the butter. Add the scallions and cook until soft, 3 or 4 minutes. Beat the eggs and blend in the cream, salt, and pepper. Pour the egg mixture into the skillet and cook, stirring constantly, until the eggs are almost done. Stir in the rice and cook until it is heated through, about 5 minutes.

BREADS

Cornbread

YIELD: 6 SERVINGS

The close-fisted stinginess that fed the poor slave on coarse cornmeal and tainted meat . . . wholly vanished on approaching the sacred precincts of the Great House itself. . . . Immense wealth and its lavish expenditures filled the Great House with all that could please the eye and tempt the taste. —Frederick Douglass, *Life and Times of Frederick Douglass*, 1892

Slave cooks learned how to make all manner of breads and other nourishing dishes out of their ration of cornmeal.

⅓ cup vegetable shortening
½ cup yellow cornmeal
½ cup all-purpose flour
3 teaspoons baking powder
1 egg, beaten
⅓ cup water
½ teaspoon salt
⅓ cup sugar
⅔ cup evaporated milk

Preheat the oven to 400 degrees.

In a heavy cast-iron skillet over moderate heat, melt the shortening. In a large mixing bowl, combine the remaining ingredients. Mix half the melted shortening into the batter, leaving the remaining half in the skillet. While the shortening in the skillet is still hot, pour in the batter. Bake the cornbread for 15 minutes, or until the top is brown and the sides crisp. (If you do not want to put the skillet in the oven, transfer the shortening and batter to an 8-inch pan to bake.)

Crackling Cornbread

YIELD: 4 TO 6 SERVINGS

Cracklings are a delightful addition to cornbread.

2 cups yellow cornmeal
1½ teaspoons baking powder
½ teaspoon baking soda
1½ teaspoons salt
½ cup cracklings (see page 146)
1 cup buttermilk
2 eggs, beaten
2 tablespoons bacon or ham drippings

Preheat the oven to 400 degrees.

Sift together the cornmeal, baking powder, baking soda, and salt. Add the remaining ingredients and mix well. Spread the batter in a greased 8-inch-square baking pan. Bake for 25 to 30 minutes.

Hoecakes

YIELD: ABOUT 14 CAKES

Many slaves devised a way to eat a hot meal in the short respite which was sometimes allowed at noontime. This "receipt" for hoecakes comes from a slave narrative. After you read it, you'll understand how these cornmeal cakes got their name.

> Stand in the shade near the edge of the field. Light a fire from whatever brush and twigs there may be. On the greased blade of your hoe, mix meal and water until it is thick enough to fry. Add salt, if you remembered to bring any. Lean the hoe into the fire until the top side of the bread bubbles. Flip it and brown the other side. If you do it without a hoe, you have to make suitable changes in the kitchen.

The following recipe makes "suitable changes in the kitchen" for making hoecakes.

2 cups white or yellow cornmeal
½ teaspoon salt
1 cup hot water
2 tablespoons melted shortening or bacon drippings
1 to 1½ cups cold water

In a bowl, combine the cornmeal, salt, hot water, and shortening. Add enough cold water to make the batter pour easily.

Grease a griddle or heavy skillet and set it over moderate heat. Pour about 2 tablespoons of batter on the griddle or in the skillet for each hoecake. After 3 to 5 minutes, or when the top begins to bubble, flip the hoecake with a spatula. Cook until the bottom turns a light brown. Eat immediately, as hoecakes lose their taste when reheated. Leftover cakes can be used in chicken dressing.

Hush Puppies

YIELD: 4 TO 6 SERVINGS

Hush puppies, small, spicy balls of cornbread, are rumored to have received their name when they were used to quiet hungry hunting dogs. A plate of fried fish seems mighty lonely without them.

1 cup white cornmeal
½ cup all-purpose flour
½ teaspoon salt
1 teaspoon sugar
½ teaspoon baking powder
½ teaspoon baking soda
½ teaspoon garlic powder
¼ teaspoon cayenne pepper or 2 or 3 drops of Tabasco sauce
2 scallions, including tops, minced
1 egg, lightly beaten
Milk to moisten, up to 1 cup
2 cups bacon fat or vegetable oil

In a medium bowl, combine the cornmeal, flour, salt, sugar, baking powder, baking soda, garlic powder, pepper or Tabasco sauce, and scallions. Stir in the egg. Slowly add milk until the batter is thick but will drop easily from a teaspoon.

In a frying pan, heat the bacon fat or oil until it is hot enough for deep-fat frying. Drop the batter by teaspoonfuls into the fat and fry until golden. Serve hot.

Spoon Bread

YIELD: 4 TO 6 SERVINGS

Spoon bread is light and rich, almost like a cornbread soufflé. It should be "spooned up" directly from the baking dish.

2 cups whole milk
½ cup white cornmeal
1 teaspoon salt
2 tablespoons butter
½ teaspoon baking powder
2 eggs, separated

Preheat the oven to 400 degrees. Put a well-greased 2-quart baking dish in the oven to heat.

In a medium saucepan, boil the milk. Gradually stir in the cornmeal; the mixture should be stiff. Add the salt and butter. Turn off the heat and add the baking powder. Beat the egg yolks and add them to the batter.

Beat the egg whites until stiff and fold into the batter. Pour the batter into the hot, greased baking dish. Bake for 35 to 40 minutes, until the spoon bread is firm in the middle and brown on top.

Pancakes

YIELD: ABOUT 8 6-INCH CAKES

My mother said she always knew times were hard when pancakes were served for supper. Pancakes are delicious, simple to prepare, cheap, and filling—an especially good meal if you have nine children to feed, as my grandmother did.

2 cups milk
4 tablespoons butter, melted, plus extra for greasing the pan
2 eggs, beaten
2 cups all-purpose flour
4 teaspoons baking powder
3 tablespoons sugar
1 teaspoon salt

In a bowl, combine the milk, butter, and eggs. Sift together the remaining ingredients and add to the milk mixture. Stir just until the flour is assimilated.

Heat a skillet or griddle over moderate heat. Grease very lightly with butter. Drop the batter onto the skillet or griddle by ¼ cupfuls. Cook, checking frequently, until the top side of the cake is full of bubbles and the underside is nicely browned. Turn the cake over and brown the other side.

Southern Pecan Biscuits

YIELD: ABOUT 2 DOZEN BISCUITS

Serve these biscuits with butter and pancake syrup and you'll be talking with a Southern drawl for the rest of the day. If you have leftover candied sweet potatoes or yams, they'll work fine. Just reduce the brown sugar by 1 tablespoon.

2 cups sifted all-purpose flour
4 teaspoons baking powder
1 cup cold mashed sweet potatoes
½ cup (1 stick) butter or margarine, melted
2 tablespoons packed light brown sugar
⅔ cup milk at room temperature
½ cup chopped pecans

Preheat the oven to 400 degrees.

In a bowl, combine the flour and baking powder. In a separate, large bowl, combine the sweet potatoes, butter or margarine, and brown sugar. Stir in the milk and flour mixture alternately until the dough is smooth. Add the pecans.

Briefly knead the dough on a floured surface—just 3 or 4 times. Roll out ½ inch thick. With a floured biscuit cutter, cut in 1½-inch rounds. Place the biscuits on a lightly greased baking sheet and bake for 15 minutes.

Beaten Biscuits

YIELD: ABOUT 40 BISCUITS

In Virginia of the olden time, no breakfast or tea-table was thought to be properly furnished without a plate of these indispensable biscuits.... Let one spend the night at some gentleman-farmer's home and the first sound heard in the morning, after the crowing of the cock, was the heavy, regular fall of the cook's axe, as she beat and beat her biscuit dough. —Mary Stuart Smith, *Virginia Cookery Book,* 1885

Many a slave cook started her day laboriously beating biscuit dough with the side of an ax or a heavy wooden mallet. Most recipes directed that the dough should be beaten "300 times for family, 500 for company." So when Miss Smith came to call on that gentleman farmer, the cook's work was doubled.

The food processor has eliminated the need to beat the dough with the side of an ax for hours at a time. Beating these biscuits does not make them light or fluffy. They are flaky and crisp, perfect as appetizers when split and sandwiched around thin slices of ham. They look a little different from the original version, but the taste should be about the same.

2 cups all-purpose flour
1/4 teaspoon salt
1/4 teaspoon baking soda
1 tablespoon sugar
1/4 cup shortening
1/3 cup milk

Preheat the oven to 325 degrees.

In a large bowl, sift together the flour, salt, baking soda, and sugar. Cut in the shortening with a pastry cutter or two knives, until the mixture resembles a coarse meal. Slowly add the milk. The dough should be very stiff. Knead it just until smooth, then form it into a ball.

Put the dough blade in the food processor. Divide the dough into 6 balls and put

all of them into the bowl of the food processor. Process for 2 minutes. Remove the dough from the bowl and knead lightly, rolling and folding a few times. Roll out the dough ¼ inch thick. Using a biscuit cutter or the rim of a glass, cut into 1½-inch rounds.

Grease a baking sheet and bake the biscuits for 30 minutes, or until they are brown on the bottom and tan on top. They should be crisp, flaky, and light. The biscuits can be stored in the refrigerator or freezer for up to 2 months.

Fried Biscuits

YIELD: ABOUT 1 DOZEN BISCUITS

These biscuits, known as bakes in the West Indies, are wonderful with fried chicken and can be cooked in the hot grease left in the skillet.

1 cup all-purpose flour
2 teaspoons baking powder
¼ teaspoon salt
2 tablespoons cold butter, cut into pieces
6 tablespoons milk
1½ pounds shortening or 3 cups vegetable oil

Into a deep bowl, sift together the flour, baking powder, and salt. Add the pieces of butter. Rub the flour and butter together between your fingers until the mixture resembles coarse meal. Pour in the milk and lightly toss the mixture together with a fork.

Gather the dough into a ball and place it on a lightly floured surface. Roll the dough about ¼ inch thick. With a biscuit cutter or the rim of a glass, cut the dough into 1½-inch rounds. Collect the scraps in a ball, roll them out again, and cut as many more rounds as you can, until all the dough has been used.

Melt 1½ pounds of shortening in a heavy skillet over high heat or, if using vegetable oil, pour it into the skillet to a depth of about 1 inch. Heat until it is very hot but not smoking. Fry the biscuits for 4 or 5 minutes, turning them with a slotted spatula until they are evenly browned. Transfer to paper towels to drain.

Short'nín' Bread

YIELD: ABOUT 2 DOZEN 1½-INCH ROUNDS

Mammy's little baby isn't the only one who loves short'nin' bread!

2 cups all-purpose flour, sifted
½ cup packed light brown sugar
1 cup (2 sticks) butter, at room temperature

Preheat the oven to 350 degrees.

Mix the ingredients until they form a soft dough. Place the dough on wax paper and pat to ½-inch thickness. With a biscuit cutter, cut into 1½-inch rounds. Bake on lightly greased cookie sheet for 25 to 30 minutes.

DESSERTS

Salt Pork Cake

YIELD: 1 10-INCH SQUARE CAKE

I'm sure an ingenious African-American cook made do with her slave's ration of salt pork to concoct this moist, delicious cake. The salt pork was a substitute for shortening. This cake has the taste, denseness, and texture of a fruitcake without the eggs or candied fruit.

1 cup finely minced salt pork
1 cup boiling water
1 cup molasses
½ teaspoon baking soda
1 cup sugar
1 cup raisins
1 teaspoon ground cinnamon
½ teaspoon ground nutmeg
½ teaspoon ground cloves
½ teaspoon ground allspice
3 cups all-purpose flour

Grease and lightly flour a 10-inch square baking pan and set aside. Put the salt pork in a large mixing bowl. Pour the boiling water over the salt pork and let stand until cool. Preheat the oven to 350 degrees.

To the water and pork add the baking soda, sugar, raisins, cinnamon, nutmeg, cloves, and allspice.

With a mixer on medium speed, beat the flour into the salt pork mixture 1 cup at a time until the mixture is smooth. Pour into the baking pan. Bake for 45 minutes, or until a toothpick inserted in the center of the cake comes out clean.

Tea Cakes

YIELD: ABOUT 2 DOZEN 3-INCH CAKES

These cookies were my first introduction to Southern cooking—African-American style. There are many variations of the recipe, but I like this one.

½ cup (1 stick) butter or margarine
1 cup sugar, plus extra for sprinkling the cakes
2 eggs, beaten
1 teaspoon vanilla extract
3½ cups sifted all-purpose flour
1 teaspoon baking powder
½ teaspoon salt
½ teaspoon ground nutmeg
½ cup sour cream

In a large bowl, cream the butter or margarine and sugar until fluffy and well blended. Beat in the eggs and vanilla extract. In a separate bowl, sift together the flour, baking powder, salt, and nutmeg and add to the butter mixture, alternating with tablespoons of sour cream and mixing well. Wrap the dough in plastic or sheets of wax paper and chill 4 hours or overnight.

Preheat the oven to 450 degrees. Dust a cutting board with flour and roll out the dough ¼ inch thick. Cut with a 3-inch round cookie cutter. Put the tea cakes on a greased baking sheet. Sprinkle with sugar.

Bake for 10 to 12 minutes, or until lightly browned.

Buttermilk Pound Cake

YIELD: 1 10-INCH TUBE CAKE

A hole in your britches lets in a heap of uneasiness. —Slave proverb

All the ingredients for this recipe should be at room temperature.

3 cups sifted all-purpose flour
½ teaspoon baking soda
½ teaspoon baking powder
¾ teaspoon salt
1 cup (2 sticks) butter
2 cups sugar
5 eggs, separated
1 teaspoon lemon zest
1 teaspoon almond extract
1 cup buttermilk

Preheat the oven to 350 degrees. Butter and lightly flour a 10-inch tube pan and line the bottom of the pan with waxed or parchment paper. Sift together the flour, soda, baking powder, and salt; then sift again. Set aside.

Cream the butter until soft. Gradually add the sugar and beat until the mixture is light and fluffy. Beat in the egg yolks 1 at a time until just mixed; do not overbeat. Add the lemon zest and almond extract. Beat in the flour mixture alternately with the buttermilk, starting and ending with the flour and beating well after each addition.

In a small bowl, beat the egg whites until light and fluffy but not dry. Fold the whites into the batter. Pour the batter into the tube pan. Bake about 1 hour, or until a toothpick inserted in the cake comes out clean. Cool the cake in the pan for 5 minutes. Slide a knife around the inside and outside of the pan. Turn the cake out onto a cake rack. Remove the paper carefully. Let the cake cool completely before serving.

Míchael's Lemon Chess Píe

YIELD: 1 9-INCH PIE

Chess pie is a very old and very popular dessert in the South. The ingredients are usually on hand, and it's simple to make. When my husband, Michael, has had a bad day this pie makes life sweet again.

- **4 eggs, at room temperature**
- **½ cup (1 stick) butter, softened**
- **1½ cups sugar**
- **1 tablespoon all-purpose flour**
- **Pinch salt**
- **2 tablespoons lemon juice**
- **1 teaspoon vanilla extract**
- **1 9-inch unbaked pie shell**

Preheat the oven to 325 degrees.

Cream together the eggs and butter until fluffy. Add the sugar, flour, and salt and mix well. Stir in the lemon juice and vanilla extract. Pour the filling into the pie shell and bake until the filling is set and the center is firm, about 35 minutes.

Vinegar Pie

YIELD: 1 9-INCH PIE

Long ago, lemons weren't always affordable or available. Vinegar is a surprisingly good substitute. Try it.

- **3 egg yolks**
- **1 cup sugar**
- **4 tablespoons all-purpose flour**
- **⅓ teaspoon salt**
- **2 cups boiling water**
- **¼ cup cider vinegar**
- **½ teaspoon yellow food coloring (optional)**
- **1 9-inch baked pie shell**

Meringue:

- **3 egg whites**
- **3 tablespoons sugar**
- **1 teaspoon lemon extract**
- **⅓ teaspoon salt**

Beat the egg yolks until thick. Add the sugar, flour, and salt and mix thoroughly. Gradually add the boiling water. Add the vinegar and in a double boiler cook the mixture until thickened, about 3 minutes. Add the food coloring, if desired, and pour into the baked pie shell.

Preheat the oven to 325 degrees.

Beat the egg whites, gradually adding the sugar a tablespoon at a time. Slowly add the lemon extract and salt. Beat until the meringue is stiff and glossy and stands in peaks when the beaters are removed. Cover the pie with the meringue, being careful to seal all the edges. Bake for 15 to 20 minutes, or until the meringue is golden brown.

Sweet Potato Pie

YIELD: 6 SERVINGS

The tater patch don't go on looks. —Slave proverb

- **2 cups boiled and mashed sweet potatoes**
- **1¼ cups sugar**
- **1 teaspoon lemon extract**
- **1 tablespoon vanilla extract**
- **1 teaspoon ground nutmeg**
- **3 eggs**
- **1 tablespoon cream**
- **6 tablespoons butter or margarine**
- **1 teaspoon all-purpose flour**
- **1 unbaked 9-inch pie shell**

Preheat the oven to 350 degrees.

With a mixer on medium speed, blend all the ingredients except the pie shell until smooth. Spoon the filling into the unbaked pie shell. Bake for 1 hour, or until firm.

Peach Cobbler

YIELD: 10 SERVINGS

My grandmother Willie Mae made "dumplings" for her peach cobbler out of leftover bits of pastry dough. When the peaches came to a boil, she dropped in the dumplings and sealed them under the crust along with the peaches. It was a delicious treat to spoon up the cinnamon-flavored dumplings along with the tasty peaches and crisp crust!

8 cups peeled, pitted, and sliced fresh peaches
2 cups sugar
1½ teaspoons ground cinnamon
⅔ cup water
¾ cup (1½ sticks) butter or margarine
2 teaspoons lemon juice
¼ cup all-purpose flour
Pastry for 3 9-inch pie crusts (page 229 or 230)

In a medium saucepan, combine all the ingredients except the flour and the pie crusts and bring to a boil. Simmer 5 to 10 minutes over low heat until the peaches are tender. Add a few tablespoons of the liquid from the peaches to the flour. Blend until smooth and stir the flour mixture into the saucepan.

Preheat the oven to 350 degrees.

Combine 2 pie pastries in a ball and roll out on a lightly floured board about ¼ inch thick. Put the pastry in the bottom of a lightly buttered 9 x 13 x 3-inch baking dish. Spoon in the peach mixture. On a lightly floured surface, roll the remaining pastry out ¼ inch thick and cut into ½-inch strips. Arrange in a lattice over the peaches. Bake for 35 to 45 minutes, or until the top is brown and the peaches are bubbling.

VARIATION FOR CANNED PEACHES:

Using 2 16-ounce cans sliced peaches, drained, and reducing the sugar to 1¼ cups, follow the instructions for fresh peach cobber, above. However, simmer the filling mixture just to heat the peaches through.

Bread Pudding

YIELD: 6 SERVINGS

Nothing went to waste in an old-fashioned kitchen. Stale bread was dressed up with apples and turned into a tasty dessert.

1 tablespoon lemon juice
½ cup packed brown sugar
4 sweet apples, peeled, cored, and cubed
¾ cup milk, scalded
2 eggs, beaten
4 tablespoons white sugar
½ teaspoon ground nutmeg
½ teaspoon vanilla extract
½ cup raisins
2 tablespoons butter, melted
8 slices stale white bread
1 cup bread crumbs

In a medium mixing bowl, combine the lemon juice and ¼ cup of the brown sugar. Add the apples and stir to coat. Refrigerate for 1 hour.

Preheat the oven to 450 degrees.

In a large bowl, mix the milk, eggs, white sugar, nutmeg, vanilla extract, the remaining ¼ cup brown sugar, the raisins, and the melted butter. Tear the bread into pieces and add it to the bowl. Mix well, mashing the bread. Add the apples and all the sugary liquid that has accumulated in the bowl with them to the bread mixture. Mix well. Pour the batter into a greased 1-quart casserole or 9-inch-square baking pan. Sprinkle with the bread crumbs. Cover with aluminum foil and bake for 30 minutes. Uncover and bake for 5 minutes longer, or until a knife stuck in the center comes out clean.

Rice Pudding

YIELD: 6 SERVINGS

A smart redbird don't have much to say. —Slave proverb

½ cup raisins
2 cups milk
1½ cups cooked rice
2 eggs, beaten
¼ teaspoon ground nutmeg
½ teaspoon salt
½ cup sugar

Preheat the oven to 275 degrees.

Fill the bottom of a double boiler with water and bring to a boil. In the top of the double boiler, combine the raisins and milk and cook, stirring often, for 20 minutes, or until the raisins are soft. Add the rice and cook 5 minutes. Mix in the nutmeg, salt, and sugar. Simmer for another 5 minutes, then remove from the heat. Pour the pudding into a 1-quart ovenproof casserole. Bake for 10 to 15 minutes.

DRINKS

Hot Southern Cider

YIELD: 8 SERVINGS

Apple cider, whether served hot or cold, is an old-time favorite. This recipe makes the whole house smell wonderful while it is heating. It's the perfect remedy for a cold, wintry day.

8 cups apple cider
12 whole cloves
1 teaspoon ground allspice
2 cinnamon sticks, broken into pieces

In a large saucepan over high heat, stirring constantly, bring all the ingredients to a boil. Remove from the heat as soon as the mixture comes to a boil. Strain through a fine sieve. Serve immediately.

Sassafras Tea

YIELD: 6 SERVINGS

My grandmother Willie Mae often made tea from sassafras bark. My mother remembers how pretty and refreshing the coppery-red tea was on a hot summer's day after working in the field. When my father was a child, he was given sassafras tea whenever he had a cold or was feeling "under the weather." Sassafras root is available in most natural-foods stores.

1 small bunch sassafras root, cut into chunks
6 to 8 cups water

Put the sassafras and water in a saucepan and boil until the tea is the desired strength, about 5 minutes. The root can be used for several pots of tea, and becomes stronger each time it is boiled. Sweeten to taste.

Old-Fashioned Molasses Nog

YIELD: 5 SERVINGS

Since there has been so much concern recently about ingesting raw eggs, I was happy to discover this old recipe for eggless "eggnog."

2 cups evaporated milk
2 cups ice-cold water
1/8 teaspoon salt
2 tablespoons sorghum molasses
Ground nutmeg, ginger, or cinnamon for sprinkling

Blend the milk, water, salt, and molasses and pour into glasses. Sprinkle a little nutmeg, ginger, or cinnamon, or the spice of your choice, on top.

Fruity Buttermilk

YIELD: 4 SERVINGS

I recall hearing my older friends talk nostalgically about mixing rich, piping-hot cornbread with thick, creamy, ice-cold buttermilk. They made it sound like the most delicious thing in the world, and while they were eating it, I'm sure it was. Here is another appealing buttermilk concoction.

3 cups thick buttermilk
1½ cups canned fruit juice (cherry, apricot, pineapple, peach, and grape juice all work well)
2 tablespoons sugar

Combine the buttermilk, fruit juice, and sugar, stirring constantly until the sugar completely dissolves. Chill and serve without ice.

GETTING REACQUAINTED

THE AFRICAN-AMERICAN KITCHEN

Sometimes you need to take time and get reacquainted with yourself.

—Angela Shelf Medearis

If you're like me, you probably have a kitchen full of time-saving, labor-saving, space-saving, energy-saving appliances. We're constantly buying things that are guaranteed to get us in and out of the kitchen faster than ever before. What I want to know is, why am I still tired? It seems to me that we've taken all the time we've saved and crammed in even more activities. Sometimes we're too busy to cook at all.

I'm at the point where I can't bear the sight of food that comes in a bucket or a brown paper bag with advertising on the sides. I want to eat at a table with real silverware, not in my car with Styrofoam and plastic. And I don't want to hear a commercial jingle in my head while I'm chewing. I blame this periodic rebellion against modern conveniences on my heredity. My family believes in eating well.

From time to time, I clear my kitchen countertops of all the newfangled stuff and cook the old-fashioned way. I like to get out the recipes my mother and grandmother used. No zapping, no whirring, and no beeping. I've found that taking the time to chop up some onions by hand is relaxing. (If I need to sneak in a good stress-relieving crying jag, I can blame it on the onions.)

Putting on a big stewpot, filling it with good, fresh food, and stirring and smelling the contents for an hour or so are soothing. Kneading a mound of bread dough, punching it down, and watching it rise all release tension. And a slice of good-

smelling bread, hot out of the oven and spread with butter, is like a mini-vacation for the senses.

From time to time, you need to meet with your family and friends around a dinner table loaded with home-cooked food. It's easier to forgive and forget when you're full. Every now and then, it's good to bake a cake or some cookies for someone you haven't had time to talk to in a while. Calling or sending a card is faster, but there's just something about making a special dish for a friend that erases long absences.

If you can't find time to add a "little bit of love" to your cooking, you need to order a pizza: don't cook! Nothing tastes worse than a meal that's been slapped together by someone who didn't want to cook in the first place. Good cooking is partly a skill, but it's really more of an attitude.

My family has produced a long line of excellent cooks. My great-grandmother Angeline was a wonderful cook and trained my grandmother Willie Mae to be a culinary artist. Willie Mae passed down all she knew to my mother, Angeline. The frying pan stops right there: unfortunately, my older sister, Sandra, and I weren't interested in learning to cook until *after* we had husbands and kitchens of our own. Why bother, when the most wonderful cook we both knew lived in our house? When I moved out, I remember calling my mother long distance several times a week to ask for detailed explanations about recipes I'd casually watched her prepare and enthusiastically eaten for years but never learned. My younger brother, Howard, and my baby sister, Marcia, were much wiser. They both learned to cook before leaving home.

Even though I was a lousy cook when I first got married, I really wanted to improve my culinary skills. After a number of disasters that I won't go into but that my friends and family will never let me forget, I learned to "burn" with the best of them. The highest compliment an African-American Texan can give about your cooking is to tell you that "you really put your foot in that food!" When I heard that for the first time, I felt as if I had received the Oscar of African-American culinary awards.

Now I'm a grandmother, and I've passed down many of the recipes contained in this book to my daughter, Deanna. I can't wait to get her baby daughter, Anysa, into the kitchen. Hopefully, she'll love to cook as much as she loves to eat. The recipes in this section are ones I've especially enjoyed preparing for my family. Some were given to me by friends who love to cook, and others are composed of ingredients that weren't available to my mother or grandmother. These recipes reflect my lifestyle—fast-paced but simple—and are always delightful.

SALADS AND APPETIZERS

Crab Salad with Feta Cheese Dressing

YIELD: 4 SERVINGS

Some people are your relatives but others are your ancestors, and you choose the ones you want to have as ancestors. You create yourself out of those values. —Ralph Ellison

2 pounds cooked crab meat
½ pound feta cheese, finely crumbled
½ cup mayonnaise
½ cup buttermilk
2 tablespoons sour cream
2 stalks celery, chopped
3 tablespoons chopped scallion
½ tablespoon soy sauce
2 tablespoons white-wine vinegar
¼ teaspoon chopped garlic
Salt and black pepper to taste
Lettuce

Mix all the ingredients except the lettuce together by hand. Serve on a bed of lettuce.

Hot Five-Bean Salad

YIELD: 10 SERVINGS

It is the mind that makes the body. —Sojourner Truth

8 slices bacon
⅔ cup sugar
2 tablespoons cornstarch
1½ teaspoons salt
⅛ teaspoon black pepper
¾ cup white vinegar
½ cup water
1 16-ounce can kidney beans
1 16-ounce can cut green beans
1 16-ounce can lima beans
1 16-ounce can cut wax beans
1 16-ounce can garbanzo beans (chickpeas)

In a medium skillet, cook the bacon until crisp. Remove from the pan and drain on paper towels. In the skillet combine the sugar, cornstarch, salt, and pepper with the bacon drippings. Stir in the vinegar and water. Heat the mixture to boiling, stirring constantly. Drain the beans and add them to the skillet. Cover and simmer 15 to 20 minutes. Spoon the beans into a serving dish, crumble the bacon, and sprinkle it on top.

Watercress and Cream Cheese Spread

YIELD: ABOUT 2 CUPS

For years, watercress sounded exotic to me. The name conjured up images of something elegant and imported. But my mother says that when she was growing up, watercress was known as a "wild" green. It was usually mixed in with a pot of mustard or turnip greens. Oh well, I still like the sound of the name, and this recipe. This spread is good on whole-wheat crackers or rice cakes.

1 3-ounce package cream cheese, softened
1 teaspoon Worcestershire sauce
¼ teaspoon salt
1 cup finely chopped watercress

In a small bowl, combine the cream cheese, Worcestershire sauce, and salt. Add the watercress and blend until the mixture is easy to spread.

Texas Caviar
(Pickled Black-Eyed Peas)

YIELD: 6 SERVINGS

This is a good dip for a New Year's Day celebration.

2 16-ounce cans black-eyed peas
½ to 1 cup salad oil
¼ cup red-wine vinegar
1 clove garlic
¼ cup chopped onion
¼ cup chopped green bell pepper
½ teaspoon salt
½ teaspoon black pepper

Drain the peas and put in a pan or bowl. Add the remaining ingredients and mix thoroughly. Store in a jar in the refrigerator, removing the garlic clove after 1 day. Refrigerate at least 2 days and up to 2 weeks before serving.

Pickled Beets

YIELD: 6 SERVINGS

Do a common thing, in an uncommon way. —Booker T. Washington

½ cup sugar
1½ teaspoons mustard seed
¼ teaspoon celery seed
1½ teaspoons salt
1 cup apple cider vinegar
1 16-ounce jar sliced beets, drained

In a saucepan, combine the sugar, mustard seed, celery seed, salt, and vinegar. Bring the mixture to a boil and pour it over the beets in a bowl, stirring gently until well coated. Let cool and refrigerate about 1 hour before serving.

Vinaigrette

YIELD: 1 CUP

I've learned to take "no" as a vitamin. —Suzanne De Passe

⅓ cup lemon juice
1 clove garlic, minced
½ teaspoon salt
½ teaspoon black pepper
1 tablespoon Dijon mustard
⅔ cup extra-virgin olive oil

In a bowl, combine the lemon juice, garlic, salt, pepper, and mustard. Whisk in the olive oil. If the dressing is too tart, add more olive oil.

Ambrosía

YIELD: 4 SERVINGS

If you respect yourself, it's easier to respect other people. —John Singleton

4 large oranges, peeled and cut into ¼-inch slices
2 cups shredded coconut
¼ cup sugar
Lettuce leaves
Whipped topping (optional)

Gently combine the oranges, coconut, and sugar. Chill about 1 hour and serve on a lettuce-covered platter. Garnish with whipped topping, if desired.

MAIN DISHES

Sunday Dínner Pork Chops

YIELD: 8 SERVINGS

You worry too much about what goes into your mouth, and not enough about what comes out of it.

—Leah Chase

8 pork chops, each ½ inch thick
1 teaspoon olive oil
½ teaspoon white vinegar
2 tablespoons vegetable oil
1 28-ounce can whole tomatoes, with liquid
1 cup finely chopped onion
1 bay leaf
4 peppercorns
1 tablespoon sugar
2 cloves garlic, minced
1 teaspoon salt
1 teaspoon dried oregano
1 16-ounce can string beans
1 16-ounce can whole-kernel corn
2 tablespoons vegetable oil

Trim all the fat from the pork chops, rinse, and dry with paper towels.

Combine the olive oil and vinegar and coat the pork chops with the mixture. In a deep skillet, heat the vegetable oil until it is hot but not smoking and brown the chops lightly on both sides. Remove from the oil and set aside. Add the tomatoes, onion, bay leaf, peppercorns, sugar, and garlic to the skillet. Bring the ingredients to a boil over moderate heat. Return the pork chops to the skillet, cover, and reduce the heat to low. Simmer for 15 minutes. Uncover and remove the bay leaves. Return the heat to moderate and cook for 20 minutes, stirring occasionally. Drain the string beans and corn and stir them in. Simmer for 10 minutes.

Spareribs Stuffed with Wild-Rice Dressing

YIELD: 6 SERVINGS

I love this dish because it's so simple and looks so elegant.

2 whole slabs pork spareribs, about the same length (2 to 3 pounds each)
Salt and black pepper to taste
½ cup all-purpose flour
1 teaspoon dried sage
1 teaspoon black pepper
1 teaspoon dried thyme
3 cups cooked and cooled wild rice
1 cup sliced mushrooms
1 onion, sliced
2 cloves garlic, minced
1 green bell pepper, seeded and diced
2 stalks celery, including tops, diced
1 cup boiling water
½ 10-ounce can condensed cream of mushroom soup
2 tablespoons steak sauce

Preheat the over to 400 degrees.

Trim the fat from the pork slabs and season with salt and pepper to taste. Combine the flour, sage, pepper, and thyme. Dredge the slabs in the seasoned flour until they are lightly coated.

Lay one slab so that the ends turn up in a roasting pan with a tight-fitting lid. In a small bowl, combine the rice, mushrooms, onion, garlic, bell pepper, and celery. Spread the mixture on the ribs. Place the second slab of ribs on top of the rice mixture so that the ends turn down. Fasten the slabs together with skewers.

In a small bowl, stir together the boiling water, the cream of mushroom soup, and the steak sauce until smooth. Pour over the ribs. Cover tightly and bake, basting frequently, until the ribs are brown and tender, 40 to 60 minutes.

Shrímp and Lobster Fajítas

YIELD: 6 TO 8 SERVINGS

I don't believe in failure. It's not failure if you enjoyed the process. —Oprah Winfrey

- **1 tablespoon sweet paprika**
- **1 tablespoon salt**
- **1 tablespoon garlic powder**
- **1 tablespoon onion powder**
- **¾ teaspoon black pepper**
- **¼ teaspoon Tabasco sauce**
- **½ teaspoon dried thyme**
- **½ teaspoon dried oregano**
- **2 pounds medium or large shrimp, shelled and deveined**
- **1 pound lobster meat, cut into 1-inch chunks**
- **1 medium onion, quartered and cut in large strips**
- **1 green bell pepper, seeded and cut in large strips**
- **½ cup olive oil**
- **½ cup lime juice**

In a small bowl, blend the paprika, salt, garlic powder, onion powder, black pepper, Tabasco sauce, thyme, and oregano. Combine half the spice mixture with the shrimp and the other half with the lobster. In a large skillet over moderate heat, stir-fry the onion and bell pepper in the olive oil for 2 minutes. Add the lobster and cook for 2 minutes, then add the shrimp and cook for 2 minutes. Add the lime juice and cook until heated through. Serve in flour tortillas with salsa, guacamole, and refried beans, or serve over rice or pasta.

Shrimp Gumbo

YIELD: 4 TO 6 SERVINGS

I had to make my own opportunity.... Don't sit down and wait for the opportunities to come; you have to get up and make them. —Madame C. J. Walker

2 cups fresh okra, stemmed and sliced
2 large onions, chopped
2 cloves garlic, minced
3 tablespoons bacon fat
1 4-ounce can tomato sauce
4 drops Tabasco sauce
½ pound smoked hot sausage, thinly sliced
1 bay leaf
1 teaspoon salt
4 cups water
2 pounds raw shrimp, shelled and deveined
3 cups cooked rice

In a large heavy pot, combine all the ingredients except the shrimp and rice. Cover, bring to a boil, and simmer for 25 minutes. Add the shrimp and cook another 2 to 3 minutes. If the gumbo becomes too thick, add more water. Gumbo should be the consistency of a thick soup. Serve over rice.

Crispy Baked Fish

YIELD: 4 SERVINGS

This simple recipe for baked Parmesan-coated fish guarantees that you'll be out of the kitchen in record time.

1½ pounds white fish fillets (trout, perch, catfish)
¼ cup vegetable oil
½ teaspoon salt
1 clove garlic, minced
1 cup grated Parmesan cheese
¾ cup dry bread crumbs

Wash the fillets under cold running water, pat dry with paper towels, and cut into serving pieces. In a small bowl, combine the oil, salt, and garlic. Arrange the fish fillets in a large flat dish. Pour the oil mixture over the fillets. After 10 minutes, turn the pieces.

Preheat the oven to 450 degrees.

Put the Parmesan cheese and bread crumbs on separate sheets of wax paper or on separate plates. Coat each piece of fish with cheese, then dredge in the bread crumbs. Arrange the fish on a greased cookie sheet or in a greased baking dish. Bake 10 to 12 minutes. Turn the pieces over and bake an additional 10 minutes, until the coating is crisp and golden.

Pecan Catfish

YIELD: 4 SERVINGS

I could draw a circle on a piece of paper and my mother made me feel like Van Gogh.
—Damon Wayans

- **4 catfish fillets, about ½ pound each**
- **2 tablespoons milk**
- **3 tablespoons Dijon mustard**
- **1 cup ground pecans**

Preheat the oven to 500 degrees.

In a small bowl, combine the milk and mustard. Dip the fillets into the mustard mixture. Coat the fillets with the pecans, shaking off the excess. Put the fillets on a greased baking sheet and bake for 8 to 10 minutes.

Chicken with Rosemary and Orange Sauce

Eating when you are hungry and sleeping when you are sleepy. That is the ultimate wisdom.
—Bessie Copage

- **6 boneless, skinless chicken breast halves**
- **¾ teaspoon dried rosemary, crushed between your fingers**
- **¼ teaspoon black pepper**
- **1½ tablespoons vegetable oil**
- **1 cup orange juice**
- **1 teaspoon orange zest**

Season the chicken with the rosemary and pepper. In a skillet over moderate heat, heat the oil until it is hot but not smoking and brown the chicken on both sides. Remove the chicken to a plate, pour off the fat in the skillet, and discard.

In the skillet, combine the orange juice and zest and simmer for 5 minutes, stirring occasionally. Add the chicken, cover, and simmer, stirring occasionally, for 20 minutes, or until the chicken is done and the sauce has thickened.

Barbecued Short Ribs of Beef

YIELD: 4 TO 6 SERVINGS

No race can prosper till it learns that there is as much dignity in tilling a field as in writing a poem.
—Booker T. Washington

3 to 4 pounds short ribs of beef
1 teaspoon salt
1 teaspoon black pepper
1 teaspoon dried sage
1 teaspoon dried thyme
All-purpose flour for dredging
1 16-ounce can chunk pineapple with juice
1½ cups water
2 tablespoons ketchup
3 tablespoons Worchestershire sauce
3 medium onions, chopped
1 clove garlic, minced
½ teaspoon dry mustard
½ cup packed brown sugar

Preheat the oven to 350 degrees.

Season the beef with the salt, pepper, sage, and thyme, dredge in flour, and put in a 2-quart casserole. In a saucepan, combine the remaining ingredients and simmer for 5 minutes. Pour over the beef. Cover and bake for 2½ to 3 hours, or until the meat is fork-tender, turning and basting with the sauce every 30 minutes. Remove the cover 30 minutes before the beef is done to permit browning. When done, remove the meat from the casserole and skim the fat from the sauce.

Chicken-Fried Steak with Brown Gravy

YIELD: 6 SERVINGS

This dish is a family (and Texas) favorite. Bring on the mashed potatoes!

1 egg
1½ cups water
2 pounds round steak, thinly cut into 6 serving pieces
2 cups all-purpose flour
1 teaspoon salt
1 teaspoon black pepper
1 teaspoon garlic powder
2 cups vegetable oil
1½ teaspoons steak sauce

In a medium bowl, using a fork, combine the egg and water. Dip the steak pieces in the egg and water mixture. Shake off the excess and put on a plate. Season the flour with the salt, pepper, and garlic powder and stir with a fork. Dredge the steak in the flour, shaking off any excess. Dip the floured steak pieces again in the egg and water mixture, then back into the flour and shake off the excess. Put the battered steak on a plate and repeat until all the pieces are coated. Reserve the remaining flour.

In a large skillet, heat the oil until a pinch of flour sizzles when sprinkled on top. Lay the steak pieces in the oil. Do not crowd the meat in the pan. Brown the pieces on both sides until done, 5 to 10 minutes on each side. Remove to a paper towel-covered plate and set aside in a warm place.

Poor off all the oil from the skillet except about ¼ cup, leaving as many of the brown bits from frying the steak as possible. Stir 3 tablespoons of the remaining seasoned flour into the oil. Cook over moderate heat until the flour is lightly browned and the mixture begins to thicken, being careful not to burn it. Stir in the steak

sauce. Slowly add warm water to the flour mixture, about ¼ cup at a time, stirring until the gravy is smooth and thin. Simmer the gravy over low heat about 5 minutes. Put the steaks on serving plates with a spoonful of gravy in the center of each. Serve the remaining gravy in a gravy boat or pitcher.

Meat Loaf with Tomato Sauce Gravy

YIELD: 4 SERVINGS

All my life I've had this almost criminal optimism. I didn't care what happened, the glass was always going to be half full.
—Quincy Jones

1 egg
1 pound lean ground beef
1 pound lean sausage
¼ cup prepared salsa
½ tablespoon steak sauce
1 teaspoon salt
1 teaspoon black pepper
1 small onion, minced
1 clove garlic, minced
1 green bell pepper, seeded and minced
½ cup dry bread crumbs

Tomato Sauce Gravy:

1 onion, diced
2 stalks celery, diced
2 tablespoons butter or margarine
1 16-ounce can whole tomatoes, chopped, with liquid
½ teaspoon Worcestershire sauce
¼ teaspoon Tabasco sauce

Preheat the oven to 350 degrees.

In a large bowl, beat the egg lightly. Add the ground beef, sausage, salsa, steak sauce, salt, and pepper and mix well, using your hands. Add the onion, garlic, bell

pepper, and bread crumbs and mix until well blended. Turn the meat mixture into a baking pan and pat into a rounded mound. Bake for 30 minutes.

To prepare the gravy: While the meat loaf is baking, sauté the onion and celery in the butter or margarine until tender. Stir in the tomatoes and their liquid and the Worcestershire and Tabasco sauce. Simmer, uncovered, for 10 minutes.

After the first 30 minutes of baking the meat loaf, drain the fat from the baking pan and pour the tomato gravy over the meat loaf, letting it run down the sides. Return the meat loaf to the oven. Bake for 30 minutes longer, or until done.

Easy Chili

YIELD: 6 SERVINGS

There is a use for almost everything. —George Washington Carver

1 pound lean ground beef
½ teaspoon salt
½ teaspoon black pepper
½ teaspoon ground cumin
2 to 3 tablespoons chili powder
1 cup chopped onion
1 large clove garlic, minced
½ cup chopped green bell pepper
1 to 2 tablespoons chopped fresh jalapeño pepper
1 large bay leaf
1 28-ounce can tomatoes, cut up, with liquid
1 14-ounce can tomato sauce
1 16-ounce can kidney beans or pinto beans, with liquid

In a large skillet, combine the ground beef with the salt, pepper, cumin, and chili powder. And the onion, garlic, bell pepper, and jalapeño pepper and cook over moderate heat, stirring occasionally, until the meat has browned. Drain off all the fat and add the remaining ingredients except for the beans. Bring to a boil. Reduce the heat, cover, and simmer 1½ to 2 hours, stirring occasionally. Stir in the beans and their liquid. Continue cooking until the beans are heated through.

Marcía's Passíonate Pasta

YIELD: 6 SERVINGS

My romantic younger sister dreamed up this combination for a Valentine's Day dinner.

6 Italian sausages: 3 mild, 3 spicy, 1½ pounds total
2 tablespoons olive oil
2 cloves garlic, minced
1 onion, finely chopped
1 green bell pepper, seeded and diced
½ pound medium shrimp, shelled and deveined
1 cup sliced mushrooms
3 plum tomatoes, sliced
1 teaspoon Italian seasoning
1 teaspoon sugar
½ teaspoon salt
½ teaspoon black pepper
½ teaspoon dried basil
¼ teaspoon cayenne pepper
1 8-ounce can tomato sauce
1½ pounds fettuccine, cooked

Remove the sausage meat from the casings. Roll the meat into meatballs. In a large skillet over moderate heat, heat the olive oil until it is hot but not smoking. Fry the meatballs in the olive oil until they are browned on all sides. Remove from the skillet and drain on paper towels.

Add the garlic, onion, and bell pepper to the skillet and sauté until the onion is golden brown. Add the shrimp, mushrooms, tomatoes, and seasonings and sauté for 5 to 8 minutes. Add the tomato sauce and sausage balls and simmer the sauce over low heat for 30 minutes, stirring occasionally. Serve over the hot fettuccine.

GREENS AND VEGETABLES

When my parents moved into a new home, my mother transported her beloved turnip, collard, and mustard greens in squat wooden tubs. She moved her garden along with the rest of the household goods as if it were the most natural thing in the world. She had to have something to nurture and love, a piece of ground to tend, until a new garden could be planted.

After my visits, my mother usually gives me a brown paper sack full of greens fresh from her garden. I enjoy eating greens, but I hate to clean them—you have to examine each leaf like a skeptic checking out a used car. Greens must be soaked in a cool salt bath and rinsed several times, or eating them is like eating a mouthful of sand. However, I gladly clean vast quantities of turnip, collard, and mustard greens just for the privilege of watching my mother care for her garden.

My mother's garden is a kind of poetry. Every green, leafy row has an earthy pentameter. The lines of corn and tomato plants are all neatly rhythmical. The broccoli, tomatoes, collards, mustard greens, onions, and bell pepper plants each have a definitive marker. The rich, warm black earth gives off a wonderful smell.

I like to sit between the rows while my mother picks the greens for me to take home. She always refuses my offers of help, because she knows that both of my thumbs are black in more ways than one. I still can't tell a budding green plant from a healthy weed.

I enjoy listening to her tell me why the bugs are so bad this year, or why this or that has gone to seed so early in the season. I pretend to understand and offer polite words of sympathy in the proper places. Her voice drifts over the rows to me as I half-close my eyes and enjoy the sun. The rays warm the top of my head and the heat flows through my body. I relax as completely as if I've had a hot bubble bath.

My mother works quickly, her hands almost a blur before my half-shut eyes. The hot sun makes me drowsy. When the sack is full, she presents her offering to me with a big smile. "Ann," she says, "these are really going to be good."

I could have anything I want from my mother's garden, vegetables that I love to eat, that require little preparation. The plump, ripe tomatoes, the good, firm broccoli, and the ears of sweet corn are mine for the asking. But I know that my mother wants me to have what she loves and enjoys the most: the greens.

Mixed Greens

YIELD: 6 TO 8 SERVINGS

The most important part of good health and relief from stress is surrounding yourself with people who love you.
—Wilma Rudolph

1 bunch collard greens
1 bunch kale
1 bunch spinach
1 bunch turnip greens
1 tablespoon salt
¼ cup vegetable oil
1 clove garlic, chopped
¼ teaspoon sugar
Cayenne pepper to taste

Cut the tough stems and yellow leaves from the greens and discard. Gently rub the leaves with your fingers under warm running water. Cut the leaves into small pieces. Fill the sink with warm water and add the salt. Let the greens soak for 10 minutes. Rinse with cool water and shake off the excess, but do not dry the greens.

Put the greens and the remaining ingredients in a Dutch oven or heavy pot. No added water is needed, as greens give off their liquid. Cover and cook over moderate heat for 45 minutes to 1 hour, stirring every 15 minutes, until the greens are tender.

Kale with Tomato and Onion

YIELD: 8 SERVINGS

1½ pounds fresh kale, washed, stems and yellow leaves removed, and torn into small pieces
2 teaspoons vegetable oil
1 cup chopped tomato
¾ cup chopped onion
2 teaspoons lemon juice
1 clove garlic, minced
¾ teaspoon black pepper

Put the wet, freshly washed kale in a large Dutch oven. Cook, uncovered, over moderate heat, stirring occasionally, for 20 to 30 minutes, until wilted and tender. No added water is needed, as greens give off their own liquid.

In a large skillet, heat the oil over moderate heat until it is hot but not smoking. Add the tomato and onion and cook, stirring constantly, until the vegetables are tender, 5 to 8 minutes. Add the cooked kale, lemon juice, garlic, and pepper. Cook for 4 to 5 minutes, stirring constantly.

Sweet-and-Sour Cabbage

YIELD: 6 SERVINGS

I had ... found that motherhood was a profession by itself, just like schoolteaching and lecturing.
—Ida B. Wells-Barnett

- **1 medium head cabbage, cored and shredded**
- **¼ cup water**
- **½ teaspoon salt**
- **1 tablespoon sugar**
- **1 tablespoon all-purpose flour**
- **2 tablespoons white vinegar**
- **1 tablespoon butter**

Put the cabbage, water, and salt in a medium saucepan. Cover and simmer over moderate heat for 10 minutes. Add the sugar, flour, vinegar, and butter; mix well. Cook until the cabbage is tender, 5 to 10 minutes.

Quick and Zesty Black Beans with Rice

YIELD: 4 SERVINGS

No meat? No matter; serve this recipe over brown rice and you won't even miss the meat!

2 teaspoons vegetable or olive oil
½ cup chopped onion
½ cup chopped red or green bell pepper
½ cup diced fresh mild chili peppers like Anaheim
1 tomato, chopped
1 clove garlic, minced
½ teaspoon dried oregano
2 16-ounce cans black beans, with liquid
¼ teaspoon sugar
Salt and black pepper to taste
2 cups hot cooked brown rice

In a saucepan, heat the oil until it is hot but not smoking. Add the onion, bell pepper, chili peppers, tomato, garlic, and oregano. Cook over moderate heat until the vegetables wilt, stirring occasionally, 5 to 8 minutes. Add the beans, sugar, and salt and pepper to taste. Cover, reduce the heat to low, and simmer for 15 minutes, stirring occasionally. Serve on a bed of rice.

MICROWAVE VARIATION:

Put the oil, vegetables, and seasonings in a microwave dish. Cook on high 7 minutes, or until the vegetables wilt. Stir in the beans, cover, and cook on medium for 10 minutes.

Cabbage and Tomato Meld

YIELD: 6 SERVINGS

It is time for every one of us to roll up our sleeves and put ourselves at the top of our commitment list.
—Marian Wright Edelman

1 head cabbage, coarsely chopped
2 tomatoes, peeled, cored, and quartered
1 onion, sliced
¼ cup vegetable oil
½ teaspoon dried thyme
Salt and black pepper to taste

Rinse the vegetables in a colander. Shake out the excess water. In a medium skillet, heat the oil until it is hot but not smoking. Add the vegetables and seasonings. Cook, covered, until the cabbage is tender, about 15 minutes, stirring occasionally.

Ríce Prímavera

YIELD: 8 SERVINGS

Make some muscle in your head, but use the muscle in your heart.

—Imanu Amiri Baraka

1 clove garlic, peeled and left whole
2 teaspoons olive oil
2 cups broccoli florets
1 cup sliced zucchini
1 cup sliced mushrooms
1 medium tomato, seeded and chopped
¼ cup chopped parsley
⅓ cup reduced-calorie mayonnaise
½ cup skim milk
¼ cup freshly grated Parmesan cheese
¼ teaspoon ground white pepper
3 cups cooked rice

In a large skillet over moderate heat, cook the garlic clove in the olive oil about 3 minutes. Discard the garlic. Add the broccoli, zucchini, and mushrooms to the skillet and cook until tender-crisp, 5 to 10 minutes. Add the tomato and parsley, and cook 1 minute longer. Remove the vegetables and set aside. Add to the skillet the mayonnaise, milk, cheese, and pepper and cook over moderate heat, stirring, until smooth. Add the rice; toss to coat. Remove the skillet from the heat and stir in the vegetables.

Oven-Roasted Potatoes

YIELD: 4 SERVINGS

If you are not feeling good about you, what you're wearing on the outside doesn't mean a thing.

—Leontyne Price

2 tablespoons olive oil
2 teaspoons dried rosemary, crumbled
4 cloves garlic, minced
½ teaspoon salt
¼ teaspoon black pepper
4 medium potatoes, cut into ½-inch slices or wedges
1 medium red bell pepper, seeded and cut into 1-inch squares

Preheat the oven to 475 degrees.

Combine all the ingredients except the potatoes and bell pepper in a shallow baking pan or on a baking sheet with sides. Add the potatoes and bell pepper and toss to coat. Arrange in a single layer. Bake for 30 to 35 minutes, tossing 2 to 3 times during baking, until the potatoes are tender and lightly browned.

BREADS AND DESSERTS

Dinner Rolls

YIELD: 3 DOZEN ROLLS

A friend fixed two dozen of these rolls for me to serve with our Thanksgiving dinner. I sampled one before freezing them, then another, then another.... I had to get the recipe from her so I could fix another batch.

7 cups all-purpose flour
2 packages active dry yeast (rapid-rising is best)
2½ cups milk
½ cup sugar
½ cup shortening
2 teaspoons salt
2 eggs
½ cup (1 stick) margarine plus extra for greasing the rising bowl

In a large bowl, sift together the yeast and half the flour.

In a saucepan, combine the milk, sugar, shortening, and salt. Heat but do not boil.

Add the liquid gradually to the yeast and flour mixture. Beat the eggs and add to the mixture. Slowly add the remaining flour. Knead or mix until smooth and elastic.

Lightly grease a large bowl with margarine. Form the dough into a ball, set in the bowl, cover, and leave in a warm, draft-free area. Let the dough rise for 10 minutes (if using rapid-rising yeast) or until it has doubled in size. Punch the dough down and roll out on a floured surface, about ½ inch thick. With a 3-inch biscuit cutter, cut out circles.

Melt the margarine and brush onto the dough circles. Fold the circles in half and

place close together in cake pans, 1 dozen rolls to a pan. Let the rolls rise in a warm place until doubled in size. They need not be covered.

Preheat the oven to 400 degrees.

Bake the rolls until brown, 15 to 20 minutes. Brush the hot rolls with more melted margarine, if desired.

Toasted Butter Pecan Cake

YIELD: 1 FILLED AND FROSTED 9-INCH LAYER CAKE

I am because we are: and since we are, therefore I am. —John Mbuti

1⅓ cups coarsely chopped pecans
⅔ cup butter
1⅓ cups sugar
3 eggs
1¼ teaspoons vanilla extract
2 cups sifted all-purpose flour
1¼ teaspoons baking powder
¼ teaspoon salt
⅔ cup milk

Butter Pecan Frosting:

¼ cup (½ stick) butter
1 pound confectioner's sugar, sifted
1 teaspoon vanilla extract
4 to 6 tablespoons heavy cream
⅓ cup of the toasted pecans

Preheat the oven to 350 degrees.

Put the pecans on a baking sheet and toast for 10 to 15 minutes, stirring frequently. Watch carefully so they don't burn. Let the pecans cool.

To prepare the cake, cream the butter, then gradually add the sugar, beating until fluffy. Add the eggs one at a time, beating well after each addition; blend in the vanilla extract. Sift together the flour, baking powder, and salt; add to the creamed mixture alternately with the milk. Stir in 1 cup of the toasted pecans. Turn into 2 greased and floured 9-inch cake pans. Bake for 25 to 30 minutes, or until a knife inserted in the center comes out clean; cool thoroughly.

To prepare the frosting, cream the butter; gradually add the sugar, beating well until fluffy. Stir in the vanilla extract. Add cream until the mixture reaches spreading consistency. Stir in the remaining ⅓ cup pecans.

Fill and frost the cake with the butter pecan frosting.

Five-Flavor Pound Cake

YIELD: 1 12-CUP BUNDT CAKE

I love the way this cake looks, the way it fills the room with its wonderful aroma, and the way it tastes!

1 cup (2 sticks) butter or margarine
½ cup vegetable shortening
⅓ cup vegetable oil
3 cups sugar
5 eggs, lightly beaten
3 cups all-purpose flour
1 teaspoon baking powder
1 teaspoon salt
1 cup milk
1 teaspoon vanilla extract
1 teaspoon butter flavoring
1 teaspoon rum flavoring
1 teaspoon coconut flavoring
1 teaspoon lemon flavoring

Preheat the oven to 325 degrees.

In a large bowl, combine the butter or margarine, shortening, and oil. Add the sugar and beat well. Add the eggs and combine well. Add 1 cup of the flour, the baking powder, the salt, and ⅓ cup of the milk and mix. Add 1 more cup of the flour and mix. Add ⅓ cup more of the milk and mix. Add ½ cup of the flour and mix. Add the last ⅓ cup of the milk and mix. Add the last ½ cup of the flour and mix. Add all the flavorings and mix well. Pour the batter into a lightly greased and floured 12-cup bundt pan. Bake until a toothpick inserted in the center of the cake comes out clean, about 1 hour and 20 minutes. Remove the cake from the oven and let cool about 1 hour. Slide a knife around the edges of the cake pan and invert the cake onto a plate.

Pie Crust

YIELD: PASTRY FOR A SINGLE-CRUST, 9-INCH PIE

No matter what accomplishment you make, somebody helps you. —Althea Gibson

½ cup shortening
2 teaspoons confectioner's sugar
1 teaspoon salt
1¼ cups all-purpose flour
1 cup cake flour
4 to 5 tablespoons ice water

Cream together the shortening, sugar, and salt. Combine the 2 flours and sift over the shortening mixture. Cut the shortening into the flour until crumbly. Sprinkle ice water over the mixture and stir just to moisten. Gather up with the fingers and form into a smooth, not sticky, ball of dough. Do not overhandle.

On a lightly floured surface, roll the dough ⅛ inch thick. Transfer to a 9-inch pie pan. Trim the edges to ½ inch beyond the edge of the pan. Fold under and flute by pinching the edges. Fill the crust with a desired filling and bake according to the directions in the recipe, or bake "blind" as follows:

To bake the pie shell, do not prick the pastry with a fork. Place another pie pan inside the first to prevent shrinking or bubbling. Bake at 350 degrees for 30 to 35 minutes, or until light brown.

Quick and Easy Pie Crust

YIELD: PASTRY FOR A DOUBLE-CRUST 9-INCH PIE

Self-help is the best help. —Aesop

- **3 cups all-purpose flour**
- **1 teaspoon salt**
- **1½ cups butter-flavored shortening**
- **¼ cup plus 1 tablespoon water**
- **1 tablespoon white vinegar**
- **1 egg**

In a large bowl, blend the flour and salt and cut in the shortening. In a small bowl, combine the water, vinegar, and egg. Add to the flour mixture and mix well. Follow rolling and baking instructions for Pie Crust (page 229).

Note: This dough can be frozen. To freeze, roll in a ball and wrap well in wax paper. When ready to use, thaw completely before rolling out.

Easy Fudge Pecan Pie

YIELD: 2 9-INCH PIES

Every man got a right to his own mistakes. Ain't no man that ain't made any. —Joe Louis

3½ cups milk
¾ cup unsweetened cocoa powder
4 cups sugar
1 cup all-purpose flour
1 tablespoon vanilla extract
½ cup (1 stick) butter
½ teaspoon salt
2 cups pecans
2 unbaked 9-inch pie shells (see page 229)
Chopped pecans and/or coconut (optional)

Preheat the oven to 375 degrees.

In a medium saucepan, mix the milk and cocoa and bring to a fast simmer. Remove from the heat. In another bowl, combine the sugar, flour, vanilla extract, butter, salt, and pecans. Pour the milk and cocoa mixture over the sugar and pecan mixture. Mix well. Pour the mixture into 2 unbaked pie shells. Sprinkle with chopped pecans and/or coconut, if desired. Bake for 40 to 45 minutes, or until set.

Lemon Icebox Pie

YIELD: 1 9-INCH PIE

Before you marry keep both eyes open; after marriage shut one. —Jamaican proverb

Crust:

1½ cups graham cracker crumbs
1 teaspoon sugar
¼ cup (½ stick) butter, melted

Filling and Meringue:

3 eggs, separated
1 8-ounce can sweetened condensed milk
½ cup lemon juice
Zest of 1 lemon
6 tablespoons sugar

Combine the graham cracker crumbs, the 1 teaspoon sugar, and the melted butter. Press into a 9-inch pie plate. Chill 10 minutes.

In a bowl, beat the egg yolks with the milk until well blended. Stir in the lemon juice and zest. Pour into the pie shell.

Preheat the oven to 350 degrees.

In a bowl (not plastic), beat the egg whites until stiff. Gradually fold in the 6 tablespoons sugar. Spread the meringue over the filling. Bake for 15 minutes, or until the meringue is light golden brown. Chill well before serving.

Walnut Sweet Potato Pie

YIELD: 1 9-INCH PIE

There's no need to hurry, yet no time to lose. —Bessie Copage

2 medium sweet potatoes or yams, peeled and boiled until tender
¼ cup (½ stick) butter or margarine
1 14-ounce can sweetened condensed milk
1 teaspoon orange zest
1 teaspoon vanilla extract
1 teaspoon ground cinnamon
½ teaspoon ground nutmeg
¼ teaspoon salt
2 eggs
1 unbaked 9-inch pie shell

Walnut Topping:

1 egg
3 tablespoons dark corn syrup
3 tablespoons packed light brown sugar
1 tablespoon melted butter
½ teaspoon maple flavoring
1 cup chopped walnuts

Preheat the oven to 350 degrees.

In a large bowl, mash the hot sweet potatoes or yams with the butter or margarine until smooth. Add the milk, zest, vanilla extract, cinnamon, nutmeg, salt, and eggs and beat until the mixture is creamy. Pour into the pie shell. Bake for 30 minutes.

Meanwhile, prepare the topping: In a small bowl, mix well the egg, syrup, sugar, butter, and maple flavoring. Stir in the walnuts.

Remove the pie from the oven; spoon the topping evenly over the top. Bake for 20 to 25 minutes longer, or until the pie is firm and golden brown. Serve warm or chilled. Refrigerate any leftovers.

HOLIDAYS OF OUR OWN

AFRICAN-AMERICAN TRADITIONS

DINNER ON THE GROUNDS

Some of my mother's fondest memories are of the goodies contained in my grandmother Willie Mae's picnic basket when their Oklahoma church had its annual "dinner on the grounds." This dinner was usually held on Memorial Day. The pastor would offer up a prayer and then the men and boys would clean and weed the graves around the church while the women and girls set the long plank tables for dinner.

After the graves were clean, the women and children would decorate them with homemade crepe-paper flowers of brilliant hues. Some families would plant flowering bushes or trees near the headstones. Once the graveyard was perfectly tidy and beautifully decorated, it was time for dinner.

Each mother brought a sparkling-clean white sheet for a tablecloth. Then, as if by magic, the table would be covered with some of the finest food in Oklahoma! After an interval of concentrated eating, the families would move from table to table to sample Sister Davis's pie or Sister Caroline's potato salad. Each cook had at least one delicious "specialty" that was always in demand at church gatherings.

After dinner, the adults had a rare chance to visit, while the children played ring games, hide-and-go-seek, and stickball. Memorial Day is seldom celebrated in this manner anymore, although such observances should be revived. The foods tradition-

ally served on the church grounds are easy to pack in modern picnic baskets. This menu includes some of those "specialty" dishes from long ago.

MENU

Southern Fried Chicken *(page 138)*
Willie Mae's Green Tomato Chowchow *(page 119)*
Picnic Potato Salad *(page 122)*
Cabbage Slaw *(page 124)*
Dinner Rolls *(page 224)*
Angeline's Raisin-Pecan Pie *(page 239)*
Five-Flavor Pound Cake *(page 228)*

Angeline's Raisin-Pecan Pie

YIELD: 1 9-INCH PIE

1½ cups raisins
1¼ cups sugar
½ cup (1 stick) butter
2 eggs
1 cup pecan halves
1 teaspoon ground nutmeg
1 teaspoon ground cinnamon
1 teaspoon vanilla extract
1 9-inch unbaked pie shell

Preheat the oven to 425 degrees.

Put the raisins in a saucepan and cover with water. Boil for 10 minutes, drain, and set aside.

Cream the sugar and butter until fluffy. Add the eggs and combine well. Mix in the raisins, pecans, spices, and vanilla extract.

Pour the mixture into the unbaked pie shell. Bake until golden brown and set, about 45 minutes.

JUNETEENTH

June 19 is the date of our emancipation celebration here in Texas. On June 19, 1865, Major General Gordon Granger stood on the balcony of Ashton Villa in Galveston and read an order from President Abraham Lincoln proclaiming that all slaves were now free. The newly liberated slaves reacted in different ways to Granger's news. Some fell on their knees in prayer. Others shouted and cried for joy. African-American Texans have celebrated June 19, or "Juneteenth" for short, ever since.

President Lincoln signed the Emancipation Proclamation that freed the slaves on January 1, 1863. It seems hard to believe that it took two years and six months for the news to reach the slaves in Texas. A slave folktale says that President Lincoln sent the news from Washington by a Union soldier who rode all the way on a mule. Others believe that even though news did travel slowly, many slaveowners knew about the Emancipation Proclamation but refused to free their slaves. President Lincoln finally had to send Major General Granger and a squad of soldiers to free the two hundred thousand African-Americans who were still in slavery in Texas.

Juneteenth is celebrated in Texas in a variety of ways. In Austin, we have a parade, a beauty contest, handmade craft booths, concerts, and, of course, food and lots of it.

MENU

Jerk Pork *(page 93)*
Pasta Vegetable Salad *(page 241)*
Fruit Salad *(page 123)*
Pickled Beets *(page 199)*
Red Rice *(page 164)*
Oven-Roasted Potatoes *(page 223)*
Toasted Butter Pecan Cake *(page 226)*

Pasta Vegetable Salad

YIELD: 6 SERVINGS

1 12-ounce can vegetable juice
¼ cup finely chopped onion
3 tablespoons tarragon-flavored vinegar
2 tablespoons vegetable oil
½ teaspoon dried basil leaves, crushed between your fingers
¼ teaspoon salt
½ teaspoon minced garlic
⅛ teaspoon black pepper
3 cups cooked drained spiral macaroni
2 cups broccoli florets
2 cups halved cherry tomatoes
½ cup sliced pitted black olives

In a jar with a screw-on top, combine the vegetable juice, onion, vinegar, oil, basil, salt, garlic, and pepper. Shake until thoroughly mixed. In a large bowl, combine the remaining ingredients. Pour the dressing over the macaroni mixture and toss to coat. Cover and refrigerate at least 6 hours, tossing occasionally.

CHRISTMAS GIFT!

Simon Brown was a slave on a Virginia plantation during the 1800s. His recollections are contained in a book titled *The Days When the Animals Talked*. In the book, he gives an account of a game called "Christmas Gift." The game was played whenever two people met on Christmas morning. Instead of saying "Good morning," whoever said "Christmas gift" first got a present from the other.

The winner usually received a gift of nutmeg-flavored cookies called tea cakes, molasses taffy, sweet potato candy, popcorn, nuts, or a bottle of homemade syrup. Everyone all over Brown's plantation, both whites and blacks, surprised each other on Christmas Day with shouts of "Christmas gift!" This is a custom you may want to revive in your family. Make sure you have plenty of these traditional presents on hand just in case you aren't quick enough to shout "Christmas gift" first.

Molasses Taffy

YIELD: 10 SERVINGS

2 cups sorghum molasses
2 tablespoons butter
1 teaspoon vanilla extract

In a saucepan, boil the molasses until it hardens and leaves the sides of the pan. Remove from the heat, add the butter and vanilla extract and stir just enough to mix. Pour into a well-greased platter or shallow pan. Let stand until the candy begins to stiffen at the edges. To pull the taffy, butter your hands lightly. Take a fist-sized portion of taffy, pull it out, and fold it back repeatedly until the candy changes to a golden color, 5 to 10 minutes. When the taffy begins to harden, break it into sticks, tie it into knots, or twist it into rings.

Sweet Potato Candy

YIELD: ABOUT 36 PIECES

2 pounds sweet potatoes, peeled, boiled, and mashed
4 cups sugar
2 teaspoons lemon juice
1 teaspoon pineapple, apple, or orange juice, vanilla extract, or cinnamon, according to taste
Confectioner's sugar for dusting the candies

Put the mashed sweet potatoes in a pan and add the sugar and lemon juice. Cook over low heat, stirring constantly, until the mixture separates easily from the pan. Set aside to cool completely. Add the flavoring. Take small portions of the mixture, dust in the confectioner's sugar, and roll out into 12-inch-long sticks. Set aside to dry. Wrap in wax-paper twists.

KWANZAA

From December 26th, the day after Christmas, until the new year begins, Kwanzaa is celebrated by African-Americans. Kwanzaa was developed in 1966 by Dr. Maulana Ron Karenga, a professor of black studies at California State University in Long Beach. Dr. Karenga also established a special set of goals called the Nguzo Saba to be memorized, discussed, and acted upon during the seven days of Kwanzaa, and throughout the year. The Nguzo Saba means "seven principles" in Swahili. The first principle of Nguzo Saba is Umoja, or unity; the second is Kujichagulia, or self-determination; the third is Ujima, or collective work and responsibility; the fourth is Ujamaa, or cooperative economics; the fifth is Nia, or purpose; the sixth is Kuumba, or creativity; and the seventh is Imani, or faith.

Kwanzaa is neither a religious holiday nor one that honors a heroic person. Kwanzaa is a cultural holiday.

This is a time when African-Americans join together to honor the heritage and traditions of their ancestors. Planning for the year to come, and working on ways to make yourself a better person and your community a better community, are important parts of the holiday. Kwanzaa is a celebration of the past, the present, and the future of African-American people.

MENU

Kwanzaa Blessing Soup *(page 245)*
Sweet-and-Sour Cabbage *(page 219)*
Kale with Tomato and Onion *(page 218)*
Rice Primavera *(page 222)*
Walnut Sweet Potato Pie *(page 233)*

Kwanzaa Blessing Soup

YIELD: 6 TO 8 SERVINGS

This African blessing soup or stew was used as a way of bringing the village together in harmony and thanksgiving. Africans call one-pot meals soups, but we would probably call this a stew. It was generally part of the feast after a bountiful harvest.

1 3-pound chicken
1 teaspoon salt
1 teaspoon black pepper
¼ teaspoon crushed red pepper flakes
1 medium onion, chopped
2 teaspoons chopped parsley
6 cups water
2 teaspoons peanut oil
4 yams, peeled and cut into cubes

Put the chicken in a large pot. Sprinkle the salt, black pepper, red pepper flakes, onion, and parsley over the chicken. Add the water and oil and bring to a boil. Lower the heat, add the yams, and simmer, covered, until the chicken is tender and done, 40 to 50 minutes.

Set the chicken on a platter and surround it with yams.

Index

Ackee
  notes on, 106
  and scrambled eggs, 106
African carrot sambal, 21
African fruit punch, 61
Akara
  awon, 11
  balls/kosai (bean scoops), 11
  meatballs, 11
Almond(s)
  chicken tagine with, 32
  milk, Moroccan, 60
Ambrosia, 200
Angeline's raisin-pecan pie, 239
Appetizers
  akara
    awon, 11
    balls/kosai (bean scoops), 11
    meatballs, 11
  codfish cakes (stamp and go), 76
  eggplant, Nigerian, 12
  meat patties wrapped in pastry, 74–75
  plantain (Ghana kelewele), 10
  South African pickled fish, 8–9
  spicy Island spareribs, 92
  spinach fritters, 100
  watercress and cream cheese spread, 197
  see also Dips; Salads
Apples
  in bread pudding, 185
  in fruit salad, 123
Apricot
  juice, canned, *in* fruity buttermilk, 189
  nectar, *in* nectar punch, 114
Artichokes, beef tagine with, Moroccan, 31
Ata sauce (pepper sauce), 7
Avocados, *in* East African ham kariba, 42

Bacon
  in hot five-bean salad, 196
  in old-fashioned string beans, 149
  in red rice, 164
Baked banana custard, 110
Baked chicken with cornbread dressing, 132–33
Baked macaroni and cheese, 145
Baked rabbit, 131
Bakes, 107
Balls
  akara/kosai (bean scoops), 11
  cornmeal, Kenya steak supreme with (dodo and sima), 36–37

Balls *(cont.)*
see *also* Meatballs
Bamia (lamb with okra), 41
Banana(s)
baked, Tanzanian, 58
custard, baked, 110
in fruit salad, 123
jam, East African, 20
nectar, *in* nectar punch, 114
peanut and, punch, 113
stuffing, duck with, 90
Barbecue, Somali (moushkaki), 33
Barbecued short ribs of beef, 209
Barley lemonade, 11
Bass
in fish poached in court bouillon, 84
in grilled fish with spicy marinade, 79
Bean(s)
black
quick and zesty, with rice, 220
sweet pepper sauce for (salsa roja para frijoles negros), 68
five-, salad, hot, 196
garbanzo. *See* Chickpeas
green. *See* Green beans
kidney
in easy chili, 214
in hot five-bean salad, 196
lima
in beans and neck bones, 150
in hot five-bean salad, 196
in Southern succotash, 144
and neck bones, 150
pinto
in beans and neck bones, 150
in easy chili, 214
in West African red beans, 47
red, West African, 47
scoops (kosai/akara balls), 11
string. *See* String beans
wax, *in* hot five-bean salad, 196
see *also* Chickpeas
Beaten biscuits, 174–75
Beef
and cassava stew, East African (muhogo tamu), 26–27
ground
in akara meatballs, 11
in easy chili, 214
in meat loaf with tomato sauce gravy, 212–13
in meat patties wrapped in pastry, 74–75
in pumpkin meat loaf, 96
in South African bobotie, 34–35
for lamb, *in* lamb taushe, 25
in moushkaki (Somali barbecue), 33
in palava stew, 22
papaya, 95
short ribs of, barbecued, 209
steak
in chicken-fried steak with brown gravy, 210–11
in dodo and sima (Kenya steak supreme with cornmeal balls), 36, 37
tagine, Moroccan, with artichokes, 31
Beets, pickled, 199
Berber and Tainey sauce, 6
Beverages. *See* Drinks
Biscuits
bakes, 107
beaten, 174–75
fried, 176
pecan, Southern, 173
Black beans. *See* Beans
Black-eyed peas
in hoppin' John, 151
in kosai/akara balls (bean scoops), 11
pickled (Texas caviar), 198
Bobotie, South African, 34–35
Bread(s)
cornbread, 167–68
crackling, 168
dinner rolls, 224–25
hoecakes, 169
hush puppies, 170
injera, Ethiopian, 56
orange, 106
pancakes, 172
pudding, 185
short'nin', 177
spoon, 171
see *also* Biscuits
Breadfruit
notes on, 78
soup, 78

Breakfast casserole, 165
Broccoli
  in pasta vegetable salad, 241
  in rice primavera, 222
Brown gravy, chicken-fried steak with, 210
Butter
  oil, spicy (niter kebbeh), 5
  pecan, toasted, cake, 226–27
Butterfish, *in* fried fish, 142
Buttermilk
  fruity, 189
  pound cake, 180

Cabbage
  with cracklings, 146
  fruited, 72
  in Ghana jollof rice, 46
  slaw, 124
  sweet-and-sour, 219
  and tomato meld, 221
  in Willie Mae's green tomato chowchow, 119
Cake(s)
  codfish (stamp and go), 76
  limbo, 73
  pound
    buttermilk, 180
    five-flavor, 228
  salt pork, 178
  tea, 179
  toasted butter pecan, 226–27
Calf's liver, *in* liver and onions, 125
Camarao à Laurentia (Mozambique shrimp), 45
Candied yams, 160
Candy
  molasses taffy, 242
  sweet potato, 243
Carambola. *See* Starfruit
Caribbean marinade, 67
Caribbean stuffed red snapper, 80–81
Carrot(s)
  in metagee, 99
  sambal, African, 21
  in yataklete kilkil (Ethiopian-style vegetables), 49–50
Cassava
  beef and, stew, East African (muhogo tamu), 26–27
  notes on, 26
Casserole(s)
  baked macaroni and cheese, 145
  baked rabbit, 131
  beans and neck bones, 150
  breakfast, 165
  chicken
    with coconut sauce, 88–89
    and dumplings, 136–37
    with peaches, 139
    with rosemary and orange sauce, 208
    tagine with almonds, 32
  greens
    mixed, 217
    mustard and turnip, 156
    and okra, 158
    and turnips, 157
  hoppin' John, 151
  papaya beef, 95
  see also Stews
Catfish
  in crispy baked fish, 206
  in efo (Nigerian spinach soup), 30
  in fish poached in court bouillon, 84
  in grilled fish with spicy marinade, 79
  pecan, 207
Caviar, Texas (pickled black-eyed peas), 198
Celery, *in* picnic potato salad, 122
Cheddar cheese, *in* baked macaroni and cheese, 145
Cheese(s)
  cheddar, *in* baked macaroni and cheese, 145
  cream, watercress and, spread, 197
  feta, dressing, crab salad with, 195
  macaroni and, baked, 145
Cherry juice, canned, *in* fruity buttermilk, 189
Cherry tomatoes, *in* pasta vegetable salad, 241
Chess pie, lemon, Michael's, 181
Chicken
  baked, with cornbread dressing, 132–33
  with coconut sauce, 88–89
  in doro we't, 24
  and dumplings, 136–37
  -fried steak with brown gravy, 210–11

Chicken *(cont.)*
in Ghana jollof rice, 46
in groundnut stew, 23
in Kwanzaa blessing soup, 245
marinated, West African (yassa poulet), 38
moambe, Congo, 39
in palava stew, 22
with peaches, 139
pepper, roast, Nigerian, 40
pie, 134–35
with rosemary and orange sauce, 208
Southern fried, 138
tagine with almonds, 32
Chickpeas
in hot five-bean salad, 196
in hummus (sesame dipping sauce), 14
Chili(s)
cucumber and, salad, South African, 18
easy, 214
Chinanadzi (pineapple drink), 61
Chitlins, 126–27
fried, 127
Chorizo, *in* Puerto Rican piñon, 94
Chowchow, green tomato, Willie Mae's, 119
Cider, hot Southern, 187
Cobbler, peach, 184
Coca-Cola, *in* Southern baked ham, 140
Cocktail, orange (naranjada), 114
Coconut
cream, shrimp salad with, 70
milk
in camarao à Laurentia (Mozambique shrimp), 45
in metagee, 99
in refresco de lechosa (milk and papaya drink), 113
and pineapple drink (refresco de coco y piña), 112
sauce, chicken with, 88–89
Cocoyams, *in* metagee, 99
Cod
in codfish cakes (stamp and go), 76
in fish poached in court bouillon, 84
Codfish cakes (stamp and go), 76
Collard greens, *in* greens and okra, 158
Concombre en daube (stewed cucumbers), 98
Condiments
African carrot sambal, 21
watermelon rind pickle, 120–21
Willie Mae's green tomato chowchow, 119
Congo chicken moambe, 39
Congo green papaya soup, 29
Coo coo, 103
Corn
creamed, 152
fried, 153
pudding, 154
in Southern succotash, 134
in Sunday dinner pork chops, 201
Cornbread, 167–68
crackling, 168
dressing, baked chicken with, 132–33
Cornmeal
balls, Kenya steak supreme with (dodo and sima), 36–37
in coo coo, 103
in cornbread, 167–68
in crackling cornbread, 168
in hoecakes, 169
in hush puppies, 170
in spoon bread, 171
see also mealie meal
Court bouillon, fish poached in, 84
Crab salad with feta cheese dressing, 195
Crackling(s)
cabbage with, 146
cornbread, 168
to make, 146
Crawfish Angelique, 85
Cream
cheese, watercress and, spread, 197
coconut, shrimp salad with, 70
Creamed corn, 152
Crispy baked fish, 206
Crust, pie, 229
quick and easy, 230
Cucumber(s)
and chili salad, South African, 18
and shrimp soup, 77
stewed (concombre en daube), 98
Curry dip, Nigerian, 13
Custard, banana, baked, 110

Date and onion salad, South African, 16
Desserts
  Ambrosia, 200
  baked banana custard, 110
  fruit salad, 123
  matrimony, 109
  peach cobbler, 184
  Tanzanian baked bananas, 58
  see also Cakes; Pies; Puddings
Dinner rolls, 224–25
Dip(s)
  curry, Nigerian, 13
  hummus (sesame dipping sauce), 14
  Texas caviar (pickled black-eyed peas), 198
Dodo and sima, 36–37
Doro we't, 24
Dressing(s)
  feta cheese, crab salad with, 195
  vinaigrette, 199
  see also Stuffings
Drink(s)
  barley lemonade, 111
  coconut and pineapple (refresco de coco y piña), 112
  fruity buttermilk, 189
  hot Southern cider, 187
  milk and papaya (refresco de lechosa), 113
  Moroccan almond milk, 60
  old-fashioned molasses nog, 188
  pineapple (chinanadzi), 61
  sassafras tea, 188
  see also Punches
Duck with banana stuffing, 90
Dumplings, chicken and, 136–37
Dundu oniyeri (West African fried yams), 52

East African banana jam, 20
East African beef and cassava stew (muhogo tamu), 214–15
East African ham kariba, 42
East African spinach (mchicha wa nazi), 48
East African stuffed okra, 53
East African sweet potato pudding, 59
Easy chili, 214
Easy fudge pecan pie, 231
Efo (Nigerian spinach soup), 30
Eggplant
  appetizer, Nigerian, 12
  stew, Ghanian (froi), 28
Eggs
  in breakfast casserole, 165
  and green onions, 166
  hard-cooked
    in doro we't, 24
    in green papaya salad, 71
    in picnic potato salad, 122
    in Puerto Rican piñon, 94
  scrambled, ackee and, 103
Ethiopian fava beans (yebaqela kik we't), 55
Ethiopian lentil salad (Yemisu selatta), 19
Ethiopian injera bread, 56
Ethiopian-style vegetables (yataklete kilkil), 49–50

Fajitas, shrimp and lobster, 204
Fava beans, Ethiopian (yebaqela kik we't), 55
Feta cheese dressing, crab salad with, 195
Fettuccine, *in* Marcia's passionate pasta, 215
Fish
  baked
    crispy, 206
    Ghana, with tomato sauce, 44
    Kenyan, with spicy sauce (mtuzi wa samki), 43
  fried, 142
  grilled, with spicy marinade, 79
  pickled, South African, 8–9
  poached in court bouillon, 84
  white
    in efo (Nigerian spinach soup), 30
    in froi (Ghanian eggplant stew), 28
  see also Names of fish
Five-flavor pound cake, 228
Flounder
  in efo (Nigerian spinach soup), 30
  in fish poached in court bouillon, 84
  in froi (Ghanian eggplant stew), 28
  in grilled fish with spicy marinade, 79
Foofoo
  notes on, 54
  rice, 54
Fried biscuits, 176
Fried corn, 153
Fried fish, 142

Fried green tomatoes, 147
Fried squirrel, 130
Fritters, spinach, 100
Froi (Ghanian eggplant stew), 28
Fruit
juice, canned, *in* fruity buttermilk, 189
punch, African, 61
salad, 123
see also Names of fruits
Fruited cabbage, 72
Fruity buttermilk, 189
Fudge pecan pie, easy, 231

Garlic, sautéed, papaya shrimp with, 86–87
Ghana baked fish with tomato sauce, 44
Ghana jollof rice, 46
Ghana kelewele (plantain appetizer), 10
Ghanian eggplant stew (froi), 28
Glazed yellow turnips, 159
Grape juice, canned, *in* fruity buttermilk, 189
Gravy(ies)
brown, chicken-fried steak with, 210–11
red-eye, ham steak and, 141
tomato sauce, meat loaf with, 212–13
Green beans
in Ghana jollof rice, 46
in hot five-bean salad, 196
in new potatoes and snap beans, 148
in yataklete kilkil (Ethiopian-style vegetables), 49–50
Green bell pepper. *See* Peppers
Green onions, eggs and, 166
Green papaya salad, 71
Greens
collard
in greens and okra, 158
in mixed greens, 217
mustard and turnip, 156
and okra, 158
turnip
in greens and turnips, 157
in mixed greens, 217
and turnips, 157
see also Kale; Spinach
Green tomato(es)
chowchow, Willie Mae's, 119
fried, 147

Grilled fish with spicy marinade, 79
Griots, 91
Grits, *in* breakfast casserole, 165
Groundnut stew, 23
Guava juice, *in* African fruit punch, 61
Gullah rice, 161
Gumbo(s)
okra, 143
shrimp, 205
see also Soups; Stews

Halibut
in mtuzi wa samki (Kenyan baked fish with spicy sauce), 43
in South African pickled fish, 8–9
Ham
baked, Southern, 140
in Ghana jollof rice, 46
in greens and okra, 158
hocks
in mustard and turnip greens, 161
smoked, *in* hoppin' John, 151
kariba, East African, 42
steak and red-eye gravy, 141
Hoecakes, 169
Hog maws, *in* chitlins, 126–27
Honey-baked onions, 155
Hoppin' John, 151
Hot five-bean salad, 196
Hot peppers, fresh, notes on, 3–4
Hush puppies, 170
Hummus (sesame dipping sauce), 14

Injera bread, Ethiopian, 56
Italian sausages, *in* Marcia's passionate pasta, 215

Jam
banana, East African, 20
see also Condiments
Jefferson rice (pilau with pine nuts and pistachios), 162–63
Jerk
notes on, 93
pork, 93
Jollof rice, Ghana, 46

Kale
in mixed greens, 217
with tomato and onion, 218
Kelewele, Ghana (plantain appetizer), 10
Kenyan baked fish with spicy sauce (mtuzi wa samki), 43
Kenya steak supreme with cornmeal balls (dodo and sima), 36–37
Key lime(s)
notes on, 107
pie, 107
Kidney beans
in easy chili, 214
in hot five-bean salad, 196
Kiwi fruit, *in* fruit salad, 123
Kosai/akara balls (bean scoops), 11
Kwanzaa blessing soup, 245

Lamb
with okra (bamia), 41
taushe, 25
Lemon(s)
in barley lemonade, 111
chess pie, Michael's, 181
icebox pie, 232
Lemonade, barley, 111
Lentil(s)
salad, Ethiopian (yemiser salatta), 19
in papaya beef, 95
Lesotho mealie meal, 15
Lettuce, *in* East African ham kariba, 42
Lima beans. *See* Beans
Lime(s), Key
notes on, 107
pie, 107
Liver
calf's, *in* liver and onions, 125
and onions, 125
Lobster, shrimp and, fajitas, 204

Macaroni
and cheese, baked, 145
spiral, *in* pasta vegetable salad, 241
Mackerel, *in* fried fish, 142
Manioc. *See* Cassava
Marcia's passionate pasta, 215
Marinades
Berber and Tainey sauce, 6
Caribbean, 67
spicy, grilled fish with, 79
Matrimony, 109
Mchicha wa nazi (East African spinach), 50
Mealie meal salad, Lesotho, 15
Meatballs, akara, 11
Meat loaf
pumpkin, 96
with tomato sauce gravy, 212–13
Metagee, 99
Michael's lemon chess pie, 181
Milk
almond, Moroccan, 60
coconut. *See* Coconut milk and papaya drink (refresco de lechosa), 113
in peanut and banana punch, 113
Mixed greens, 217
Molasses
nog, old-fashioned, 188
taffy, 242
Moroccan almond milk, 60
Moroccan beef tagine with artichokes, 31
Moushkaki (Somali barbecue), 33
Mozambique shrimp (camarao à Laurentia), 45
Mtuzi wa samki (Kenyan baked fish with spicy sauce), 43
Muhogo tamu (East African beef and cassava stew), 26–27
Mushrooms, *in* rice primavera, 222
Mustard and turnip greens, 156

Naranjada (orange cocktail), 114
Neck bones, beans and, 150
Nectar
apricot, *in* nectar punch, 114
banana, *in* nectar punch, 114
punch, 114
New potatoes and snap beans, 148
Nigerian curry dip, 13
Nigerian eggplant appetizer, 12
Nigerian roast pepper chicken, 40
Nigerian spinach soup (efo), 30
Niter kebbeh (spicy butter oil), 5
Nog, molasses, old-fashioned, 188

Oil, butter, spicy (niter kebbeh), 5
Okra
  in akara awon, 11
  in coo coo, 103
  greens and, 158
  gumbo, 143
  lamb with (bamia), 41
  in metagee, 99
  stuffed, East African, 53
Old-fashioned molasses nog, 188
Old-fashioned string beans, 149
Onion(s)
  date and, salad, South African, 16
  green, eggs and, 166
  honey-baked, 155
  liver and, 125
  in metagee, 99
  in okra gumbo, 143
  tomato and, kale with, 218
  in Willie Mae's green tomato chowchow, 119
  in yataklete kilkil (Ethiopian-style vegetables), 49–50
Orange
  bread, 106
  cocktail (naranjada), 114
  in fruit salad, 123
  juice, *in* African fruit punch, 61
  in matrimony, 109
  rice, 101
  rosemary and, sauce, chicken with, 208
  salad, 17
Orange roughy, *in* fish poached in court bouillon, 84
Oven-roasted potatoes, 223

Palava stew, 22
Pancakes, 172
Papaya(s)
  beef, 95
  green
    salad, 71
    soup, Congo, 29
  juice, *in* African fruit punch, 61
  milk and, drink (refresco de lechosa), 113
  notes on, 29, 71
  shrimp with sautéed garlic, 86–87
Pasta
  passionate, Marcia's, 215
  vegetable salad, 241
Pastry
  meat patties wrapped in, 74–75
  see *also* Pie crust
Patties, meat, wrapped in pastry, 74–75
Peach(es)
  chicken with, 139
  cobbler, 184
  juice, canned, *in* fruity buttermilk, 189
Peanut(s)
  and banana punch, 113
  butter
    in Congo chicken moambe, 39
    in dodo and sima (Kenya steak supreme with cornmeal balls), 36–37
    in groundnut stew, 23
    in peanut and banana punch, 113
  in twice-baked sweet potatoes, 97
  see *also* groundnuts
Peas
  black-eyed. *See* Black-eyed peas
  pigeon, and rice, 102
Pecan
  biscuits, Southern, 173
  butter, toasted, cake, 226–27
  catfish, 207
  fudge, pie, easy, 231
  raisin-, pie, Angeline's, 239
Pepper(s)
  chicken, roast, Nigerian, 40
  green bell
    in Willie Mae's green tomato chowchow, 119
    in yataklete kilkil (Ethiopian-style vegetables), 49–50
  hot, fresh, notes on, 3–4
  red bell
    in ata sauce (pepper sauce), 7
    in Willie Mae's green tomato chowchow, 119
  sauce (ata sauce), 7
  sweet, sauce for black beans (salsa roja para frijoles negros), 68
Perch, *in* crispy baked fish, 206
Pickle, watermelon rind, 120–21
Pickled beets, 199
Pickled black-eyed peas (Texas caviar), 198

Pie(s)
chess, lemon, Michael's, 181
chicken, 134–35
crust, 229
quick and easy, 230
fudge pecan, easy, 231
Key lime, 107
lemon icebox, 232
raisin-pecan, Angeline's, 239
sweet potato, 183
walnut, 233–34
vinegar, 182
Pigeon peas and rice, 102
Pig's feet in tomato sauce, 129
Pilau with pine nuts and pistachios (Jefferson rice), 162–63
Pimentos
in green papaya salad, 71
in salsa rota para frijoles negros (sweet pepper sauce for black beans), 68
Pineapple
in barbecued short ribs of beef, 209
coconut and, drink (refresco de coco y piña), 112
in fruited cabbage, 72
juice, *in* African fruit punch, 61
canned, *in* fruity buttermilk, 189
rice pudding, 108
Pine nuts and pistachios, pilau with (Jefferson rice), 162–63
Piñon, Puerto Rican, 94
Pinto beans. *See* Beans
Pistachios
in gullah rice, 161
pine nuts and, pilau with (Jefferson rice), 162–63
Plantain(s)
appetizer (Ghana kelewele), 10
in limbo cakes, 73
in metagee, 99
in Puerto Rican piñon, 94
Porgies, *in* fried fish, 142
Pork
chops, Sunday dinner, 201
in griots, 91
jerk, 93
neck bones, *in* beans and neck bones, 150
salt
cake, 178–79
in greens and turnips, 157
sausage, *in* Puerto Rican piñon, 94
spareribs
spicy Island, 92
stuffed with wild-rice dressing, 202–03
Potatoes
in metagee, 99
new, and snap beans, 148
oven-roasted, 223
salad, picnic, 122
sweet. *See* Sweet potatoes
in yataklete kilkil (Ethiopian-style vegetables), 49–50
Pound cake
buttermilk, 180
five-flavor, 228
Pudding(s)
bread, 185
corn, 154
rice, 186
pineapple, 108
sweet pudding, East African, 59
Puerto Rican piñon, 94
Pumpkin
in lambe taushe, 25
meat loaf, 96
in metagee, 99
Punch(es)
fruit, African, 61
nectar, 114
peanut and banana, 113

Quick and zesty black beans with rice, 220

Rabbit, baked, 131
Raisin-pecan pie, Angeline's, 239
Red beans, West African, 47
Red bell peppers. *See* Peppers
Red-eye gravy, ham steak and, 141
Red rice, 164
Red snapper
in Ghana baked fish with tomato sauce, 44
stuffed, Caribbean, 80–81
Refresco de coco y piña (coconut and pineapple drink), 112

Refresco de lechosa (milk and papaya drink), 113
Rice
  in eggs and green onion, 166
  foofoo, 54
  gullah, 161
  Jefferson (pilau with pine nuts and pistachios), 162–63
  jollof, Ghana, 46
  orange, 101
  pigeon peas and, 102
  primavera, 222
  pudding, 186
    pineapple, 108
  quick and zesty black beans with, 220
  red, 164
  salad, 69
  wild-, dressing, spareribs stuffed with, 202–03
Rosemary and orange sauce, chicken with, 208

Salad(s)
  ambrosia, 200
  cabbage slaw, 124
  crab, with feta cheese dressing, 195
  cucumber and chili, South African, 18
  date and onion, South African, 16
  five-bean, hot, 196
  fruit, 123
  fruited cabbage, 72
  green papaya, 71
  lentil, Ethiopian (yemiser selatta), 19
  mealie meal, Lesotho, 15
  orange, 17
  pasta vegetable, 241
  pickled beets, 199
  potato, picnic, 122
  rice, 69
  shrimp, with coconut cream, 70
Salmon, *in* fish poached in court bouillon, 84
Salsa roja para frijoles negros (sweet pepper sauce for black beans), 68
Salt pork
  cake, 178
  in greens and turnips, 157
Sambal, carrot, Africa, 21
Sassafras tea, 188
Sauce(s)
  ata (pepper sauce), 7
  Berber and tainey, 6
  coconut, chicken with, 88–89
  dipping, sesame (hummus), 14
  niter kibbeh (spicy butter oil), 5
  pepper (ata sauce), 7
  rosemary and orange, chicken with, 208
  spicy, Kenyan baked fish with (mtuzi wa samki), 43
  sweet pepper, for black beans (salsa roja para frijoles negros), 68
  tomatillo, swordfish, with, 82
  tomato
    Ghana baked fish with, 44
    gravy, meat loaf with, 212–13
    pigs' feet in, 129
  see also Gravies
Sausage(s)
  chorizo, *in* Puerto Rican piñon, 94
  Italian, *in* Marcia's passionate pasta, 215
  in meat loaf with tomato sauce gravy, 212–13
  pork, *in* Puerto Rican piñon, 94
  smoked hot, *in* shrimp gumbo, 205
Scallions. *See* Green onions
Sesame
  dipping sauce (hummus), 14
  seeds
    notes on, 14
    spinach and (Ugandan spinach and simsim), 51
Short'nin' bread, 177
Short ribs of beef, barbecued, 209
Shrimp
  cucumber and, soup, 77
  in froi (Ghanian eggplant soup), 28
  in groundnut stew, 23
  gumbo, 205
  and lobster fajitas, 204
  in Marcia's passionate pasta, 215
  Mozambique (camarao à Laurentia), 45
  papaya, with sautéed garlic, 86–87
  salad with coconut cream, 70
Sima, dodo and, 36–37
Simsim, Ugandan spinach and (spinach and sesame seeds), 51
Slaw, cabbage, 124
Smoked hot sausage, *in* shrimp gumbo, 205

Snacks
limbo cakes, 73
see also Appetizers
Snap beans
new potatoes and, 148
see also Green beans; String beans
Sole
in efo (Nigerian spinach soup), 30
in fish poached in court bouillon, 84
in froi (Ghanian eggplant stew), 28
Somali barbecue (moushkaki), 33
Soup(s)
breadfruit, 78
cucumber and shrimp, 77
green papaya, Congo, 29
Kwanzaa blessing soup, 245
spinach, Nigerian (efo), 30
see also Gumbos; Stews
South African bobotie, 34–35
South African cucumber and chili salad, 18
South African date and onion salad, 16
South African pickled fish, 8–9
Southern baked ham, 140
Southern fried chicken, 138
Southern pecan biscuits, 173
Southern succotash, 144
Spareribs
spicy Island, 92
stuffed with wild-rice dressing, 202–03
Spicy butter oil (niter kebbeh), 5
Spicy Island spareribs, 92
Spinach
Easy African (mchicha wa nazi), 50
fritters, 100
in lamb taushe, 25
in mixed greens, 217
and sesame seeds (Ugandan spinach and simsim), 51
and simsim, Ugandan (spinach and sesame seeds), 51
soup, Nigerian (efo), 30
Spiral macaroni, *in* pasta vegetable salad, 241
Spoon bread, 171
Spread, watercress and cream cheese, 197
Squirrel, fried, 130
Stamp and go (codfish cakes), 76
Starfruit
in matrimony, 109
notes on, 109
Steak(s)
chicken-fried, with brown gravy, 210–11
ham, and red-eye gravy, 141
supreme, Kenya, with cornmeal balls (dodo and sima), 36–37
Stewed cucumbers (concombre en daube), 98
Stew(s)
bamia (lamb with okra), 41
chitlins, 126–27
crawfish Angelique, 85
doro we't, 24
East African beef and cassava (muhogo tamu), 26–27
eggplant, Ghanian (froi), 28
groundnut, 23
lamb taushe, 25
palava, 22
pig's feet in tomato sauce, 128
Southern succotash, 144
tripe, 128
see also Casseroles; Gumbos
String beans
in new potatoes and snap beans, 148
old-fashioned, 149
in Sunday dinner pork chops, 201
see also Green beans
Stuffing(s)
banana, duck with, 90
cornbread dressing, baked chicken with, 132–33
Succotash, Southern, 144
Sunday dinner pork chops, 201
Sweet pepper sauce for black beans (salsa roja para frijoles negros), 68
Sweet potato(es)
candy, 243
in metagee, 99
pie, 183
pudding, East African, 59
in Southern pecan biscuits, 173
twice-baked, 97
walnut, pie, 233
for yams
in candied yams, 160
in dundu oniyeri (West African fried yams), 52

Sweet-and-sour cabbage, 219
Swordfish with tomatillo sauce, 82

Taffy, molasses, 242
Tagine(s)
  beef, Moroccan, with artichokes, 31
  chicken, with almonds, 32
Tainey, Berber and, sauce, 6
Tanzanian baked bananas, 58
Tea
  cakes, 179
  sassafras, 188
Texas caviar (pickled black-eyed peas), 198
Toasted butter pecan cake, 226–27
Tomatillo(s)
  notes on, 82
  sauce, swordfish with, 82
Tomato(es)
  in ata sauce (pepper sauce), 7
  cabbage and, meld, 221
  cherry, *in* pasta vegetable salad, 241
  in concombre en daube (stewed cucumbers), 98
  in East African ham kariba, 42
  in easy chili, 214
  in Ghana jollof rice, 46
  green
    chowchow, Willie Mae's, 119
    fried, 147
  in okra gumbo, 143
  and onion, kale with, 218
  in red rice, 164
  in rice primavera, 222
  in salsa roja para frijoles negros (sweet pepper sauces for black beans), 68
  sauce
    Ghana baked fish with, 44
    gravy, meat loaf with, 212–13
    pig's feet in, 129
  in Southern succotash, 144
Tripe, 128
Trout
  in crispy baked fish, 206
  in fish poached in court bouillon, 84
Tuna, *in* fish poached in court bouillon, 84
Turnip(s)
  greens
    in greens and turnips, 157
    mustard and, 156
  greens, and, 157
  yellow glazed, 159
Twice-baked sweet potatoes, 97

Ugandan spinach and simsim (spinach and sesame seeds), 51

Vegetable(s)
  Ethiopian-style (yataklete kilkil), 48–49
  pasta, salad, 241
  see also Names of vegetables
Vinaigrette, 199
Vinegar pie, 182

Walnut(s)
  in fruit salad, 123
  sweet potato pie, 233
Watercress and cream cheese spread, 197
Watermelon rind pickle, 120–21
Wax beans, *in* hot five-bean salad, 196
West African fried yams (dundu oniyeri), 52
West African marinated chicken (yassa au poulet), 38
West African red beans, 47
Whitings, *in* fried fish, 142
Wild-rice dressing, spareribs stuffed with, 202–03
Willie Mae's green tomato chowchow, 119

Yams
  candied, 160
    fried, West African (dundu oniyeri), 52
  in Kwanzaa blessing soup, 245
  notes on, 52
Yassa au poulet (West African marinated chicken), 38
Yataklete kilkil (Ethiopian-style vegetables), 48–49
Yebaqela kik we't (Ethiopian fava beans), 55
Yellow turnips, glazed, 159
Yemiser selatta (Ethiopian lentil salad), 19

Zucchini, *in* rice primavera, 222